Praise for PLAYFUL

"I'm very grateful for the contributions that Carmen has made to the IFS community, and this book is no exception! *Playful Parts Work* skillfully demonstrates how IFS and play therapy can be combined to help our youngest clients thrive. Children instinctively understand parts—they live with their angry parts, scared parts, and playful parts every day. This book shows us how play therapy can become a bridge to help children access their Self-energy and develop healthy relationships with all their parts, even the ones that carry big feelings or painful experiences. Through case studies and practical exercises, this book offers concrete tools that honor both the developmental needs of young people and the healing wisdom of IFS."

–Richard C. Schwartz, PhD, founder of Internal Family Systems

"*Playful Parts Work* is a treasure of information about both play therapy and applying the IFS model to it. Carmen is an expert in both and her passion for working with a younger population and the IFS model is evident in her writing, making *Playful Parts Work* not only clinically helpful but a joy to read. The book is a wonderful combination of theory, case examples, and activities that give a clear roadmap for how beginners and experienced play therapists alike can apply the skills. However, this book isn't just helpful for those who currently or hope to work with children and adolescents— the concepts can also be used with adult clients to enrich their work. So, I highly recommend *Playful Parts Work* to everyone, whether you work with children, adolescents, or adults."

—Pamela K. Krause, LCSW, IFS Institute Senior Lead Trainer

"Carmen begins this book by describing her journey learning about IFS. I admire her naming her initial ambivalence and how she addressed it by immersing herself in learning more about this approach. It is clear that Carmen found one of her passions as she incorporated IFS into her play therapy practice, honing the art of promoting playful parts work in her clients in a truly integrative way that highly prioritizes self-discovery, reflection, and earnest interest in symbols and how our unconscious selects them. Therapists will love seeing how Carmen utilizes metaphors and symbols (in and out of the sand tray) to encourage client reflection and inevitable acceptance of all—recognized and unrecognized, owned and disowned—parts of self. The client is guided to spend time with their externalized symbols, deepening their connection, exploring, creating, and developing empathy toward all their parts. The book is replete with clinical examples; I felt I was eavesdropping on highly effective therapy sessions. The merging of play therapy, expressive arts, and playful parts work, based on IFS principles, is smooth and congruent. I believe therapists will find this book innovative and inspiring in many ways—it provides information on the integration of IFS, play therapy models, sand therapy, LEGO therapy, and the directive-nondirective continuum of responses. Brava, Carmen Jimenez-Pride. I learned a lot!"

—**Eliana Gil, PhD,** founder and partner, Gil Institute for Trauma Recovery and Education

"*Playful Parts Work* is an accessible guidebook for clinicians looking to bring IFS into their work with kids. Carmen's real-life examples are relatable, and her creative activities make parts work feel playful and deeply meaningful. As someone who specializes in IFS and EMDR integration, I appreciate the synergy of her approach and how easy it is to bring into sessions right away."

—**Kendhal Hart, PsyD, LPCC,** EMDRIA Approved Consultant
and Trainer and IFS Approved Clinical Consultant

"As a play therapist newly introduced to Internal Family Systems and parts work, *Playful Parts Work* has been an invaluable resource. Carmen skillfully distills the core concepts of IFS into practical, accessible strategies specifically tailored for working with children. She bridges the gap between theory and practice with clarity and care, offering concrete ways to engage a child's protective system through play. This book is an essential guide for any play therapist seeking to deepen their understanding of parts work and support children in navigating their inner world."

—Dr. Stephanie McMillan, LAC, RPT, LPC, NCC

"Carmen Jimenez-Pride's book fills a crucial gap in the field, offering a wealth of knowledge that has been long overdue. She is a true trailblazer, seamlessly integrating Internal Family Systems (IFS) and play therapy— two powerful modalities that deeply complement one another. The field is incredibly fortunate to have her expertise and wisdom, and I am thrilled to incorporate her groundbreaking work into my training."

—Stefani Misiph, LMHC, RPT-S, IFS Certified Therapist and founder of the Misiph Center for Therapy and Training

"As a therapist who primarily works with adults, I wasn't sure how play therapy or parts work would fit into my practice until I read *Playful Parts Work*. Carmen's thoughtful and skillful approach opened my eyes to how accessible, meaningful, and even joyful this work can be, not just for children but for the younger parts living inside every adult client I meet. This book breaks down the foundational concepts of Internal Family Systems in a clear, engaging, and approachable way, while offering practical, playful strategies I can immediately use to help my clients connect with their protective parts and wounded younger selves. *Playful Parts Work* is an essential resource for any clinician ready to invite curiosity, creativity, and compassion into the therapy room, whether you're working with kids, adults, or the child parts we all carry."

—Natalie Pride, LCSW

PLAYFUL PARTS WORK

An Introductory Guide
to Integrating **Play Therapy** with
Internal Family Systems (IFS)

Carmen Jimenez-Pride, LCSW, RPT-S™

Published by
PESI Publishing, Inc.
3839 White Ave
Eau Claire, WI 54703

Cover and interior design by Emily Dyer
Editing by Molly Gage

ISBN 9781683738497 (print)
ISBN 9781683738503 (ePUB)
ISBN 9781683738510 (ePDF)

PESI Publishing
pesipublishing.com

TABLE OF CONTENTS

CHAPTER 1

Introduction to Playful Parts

found my way to clinical therapy—and Playful Parts—through Child Protection Services (CPS). That's where I started my career as a clinical social worker, and that's where I saw that kids in my community not only needed experienced and specialized approaches to processing their traumas; they also needed the stability and commitment of continuous care. I felt called to provide this work. Simply put, there were too many children who needed clinical services while involved with CPS, and too few people able to provide these services. Although there are a variety of structural reasons for this, I was already invested in the work and its stakeholders, and I wanted to do more to help its kids.

My social work education was focused on macro work with communities and organizations, so I had very little knowledge about working directly with children. As I began to move toward becoming a therapist, I focused my research and training on clinical work with kids. Time and time again, I found myself looking to the resources at the Association for Play Therapy website. Play therapy really appealed to me, partly because it seemed like such a natural way to connect with kids. I soon became a member, orienting my training and supervision toward working with kids, and increasing my skill set to offer the kinds of therapeutic services lacking in my community.

While attending play therapy trainings, I couldn't help but notice that there were few African American therapists attending training events. Frequently, I was the only African American therapist in the room. I didn't like this experience, but my concern had less to do with feeling isolated and marginalized and more to do with what this meant for kids seeking therapy. From my perspective, the number of kids of color involved in the child welfare system who needed services was only increasing. This insight began to shift my professional goals, and I decided to become a Registered Play Therapist™ with a goal of bringing play therapy to more clinicians of color. It's no coincidence that I started my private practice in a community that did not have many play therapists and, as far as I knew, had no play therapists of color.

The more I learned, the more reasons I found to love play therapy. I believe—then as now — that play therapy allows us to step out of the box of traditional talk therapy methods and try out methods that are more creative and less constrained by conversational modes. I also believe that creativity is rooted in our earliest efforts to communicate with one another and that it can therefore unite us with our clients and motivate shared work. One of my favorite play therapy quotes comes from Garry Landreth, founder of the Center for Play Therapy at the University of North Texas. According to Landreth, "Toys are children's words and play is their language." Like the earliest play therapists, Landreth defines play as the child's natural method of communication. Play allows kids, and sometimes adults too, to tell their stories in ways that feel right to them, even when they do not have the words to express themselves.

Play therapy has been around in different iterations since the 1940s, but its methods have always been characterized by efforts to create a container for children to build their confidence and to explore and express themselves by activating their imagination and having fun. I've seen the effects of these methods firsthand, over and over again. In fact, I can still remember incorporating play activities into my interactions with children while working in CPS. During my first meeting with a new client, a 7-year-old boy, he was scared to talk to me because I was a social worker and a new adult who seemed to suddenly appear during a difficult time in his life. He wasn't interested in coloring, which was the typical method child welfare social workers used to interact with children. He didn't want to interact. However, when I pulled out Optimus Prime and Bumblebee Transformer figurines, his face brightened up, and he began to tell me about the movies he used to watch with his dad. The toys did more than ease the interaction too. He was still scared to say what happened in his home, so he used the toys as a prop to play the story out.

Play therapy has also impacted me and the way I show up for myself, my family, my friends, my colleagues, and the wider community. By routinely tapping into my own creative roots, I feel like I've unlocked new pathways to empathy, self-awareness, and connection that shape my daily interactions and personal growth. But play is also a grounding force that allows me to approach challenges with curiosity rather than judgment. It has taught me the importance of self-compassion and has encouraged me to embrace my own imperfections as opportunities for growth. I find myself more patient and forgiving, not only with others but with my own journey.

In my family life, play therapy has redefined how I communicate and bond with my family members. Through playful engagement and creative expression, I have cultivated deeper connections with my loved ones, fostering environments where vulnerability and authenticity thrive—whether it's through laughter, storytelling, or shared artistic experiences. Among friends, I have become a better listener and more attuned to their emotional landscapes. I know that play therapy has heightened my ability to hold space for others and to recognize the significance of nonverbal communication and the power of shared experiences. The shift has led to more meaningful and supportive relationships.

In professional settings, my ongoing work with play therapy means I show up in my role with a renewed sense of creativity and flexibility. Play therapy has strengthened my ability to navigate complex dynamics, encouraging innovative problem-solving and fostering a culture of collaboration with all of my clients, whether or not they benefit from explicit play therapy methods. I'm also more attuned to the diverse needs of my colleagues and find myself increasingly capable of embracing different perspectives with an open heart and mind.

My work in play therapy has also changed my interactions at the community level. It has only further stimulated my desire to advocate for spaces of healing and creativity, particularly for marginalized groups. I actively seek opportunities to contribute, whether through workshops, mentorship, or community events that promote mental wellness and inclusivity. This work aligns with my commitment to supporting BIPOC (Black, Indigenous, and People of Color) play therapists and amplifying their voices.

But I'm not just a play therapist. I'm also an expert and practitioner of the Internal Family Systems model, or IFS. When I began to work with IFS, it wasn't because I was tired of play therapy or because I felt that I had squeezed all the value out of play therapy tools. In fact, when I first learned about the IFS model back in 2018, I was a little skeptical of its utility. At first, it felt too complicated to consider integrating into my playroom. However, it seemed to cross my computer screen more and more often. Once, while researching therapy models focused on addressing trauma, I consulted with some therapist groups of which I'm a member and found other therapists were also talking about IFS. When I saw an opportunity to listen to a therapist's live chat, I tuned in. Her experience with the model inspired me, and I decided to find out for myself if IFS could help some of my hardest-to-reach young clients.

At the time, I still saw incredible results from play therapy. But I had to admit that I also worked with a small group of clients—adults and kids—who wanted to give up this sort of therapeutic work. Some were overwhelmed by what they perceived as the demands of play therapy, while others felt like they weren't making progress in their treatment plan. At the same time, I also worked with clients who seemed to be so focused on their diagnosis that they were unable to differentiate their diagnosis from other aspects of their identity. These clients also didn't seem to experience the same gains from play therapy as others.

I thought IFS might be able to reach these clients, but I proceeded with caution. Although my interest in the model had only sharpened after my exposure to it, my skepticism was also provoked. I found some of the model's concepts, such as the *healing steps*, to be somewhat ritualistic, and almost even new-age in format. Also, IFS seemed to have a lot of moving parts. I wasn't sure it could be integrated into my current work, and I wasn't convinced it was as effective as other models I'd used. Despite these reservations, something about it continued to intrigue me. I couldn't walk away from my curiosity or my own sense that IFS might be useful to my clients, particularly those whose treatment had stalled.

The more time I spent learning about IFS, the more I realized I needed more substantive training to make any real decisions about integrating it into my work. I signed up for a training for coaches, and on the very first day of training, the model started to come together and make sense to me. I finally *got* it, and I learned that some of my skepticism was valid. It's true—IFS *is* made up a lot of moving parts. But that's because people— you, me, and everyone we know—are made up of many moving parts. Yes, we've got our organs and limbs, but we also carry within us, internally, different embodiments of the experiences we've had, particularly traumatic experiences, at different stages of our lives, especially childhood. These different parts make up a family system, which works in conjunction with our singular Self to ensure our literal, figural, and even spiritual survival. Sometimes this internal family system is harmonious. Sometimes, it's anything but. IFS teaches us that when we identify, understand, and relate to our different parts, we bring these parts into accordance with each other and with our Self—our essence—which peaceably strengthens our internal system and enables us to interact with ourselves and with the world more comfortably and more authentically.

After completing this IFS training, I felt absolutely sure that the model had the potential to enact real change in my clients' lives. I was motivated to begin the kind of comprehensive training that could teach me the entire model. Meanwhile, I assigned myself a crash course to quickly learn as much as possible from books like *Introduction to the Internal Family Systems Model* by Richard Schwartz (2023) and *Internal Family Systems Skills Training Manual* by Frank Anderson, Martha Sweezy, and Richard Schwartz (2017).

These books fueled an energy within me that was reflected back to me from the very first day of my Level 1 IFS training. Although my previous training had been incredibly helpful, I wouldn't say it had been characterized by *passion*. This more comprehensive training was different.

It was conducted retreat-style, which meant that all of the participants—including me—believed so much in the model and the necessity to be trained in it that we were willing to spend two weeks away from our practices, our families, and our lives in exchange for education about it. From the first day on, I felt united in purpose with my fellow trainees. Watching the model demonstrated live by enthusiastic, dedicated staff and trainers, I knew with all my parts that IFS was the missing piece to my clinical work.

Critically, IFS is *not* diagnosis driven. As I've already described, for some clients a diagnosis can pose an obstacle to treatment. A client with a diagnosis of attention-deficit/hyperactivity disorder (ADHD), for example, may experience their emotions, feelings, thoughts, and actions through the lens of distraction, impulsivity, or hyperactivity. They may interpret their challenges as inherent flaws, leading to internalized frustration or low self-esteem. Or they may begin to identify so strongly with their diagnosis that it becomes a defining feature of their self-concept. This identification can provide comfort and a sense of belonging within communities or support groups but may inadvertently hinder therapeutic progress. A client with ADHD might, for instance, attribute all the difficulties they face solely to ADHD, overlooking other contributing factors such as environment, relationships, or emotional patterns.

Additionally, a client who closely identifies with their diagnosis may even consider treatment efforts to be ineffective or even unwelcome, perhaps because they threaten the client's understanding of themselves. For example, Jamie, a client who had been diagnosed with ADHD in early adolescence, often expressed that their impulsivity and disorganization were intrinsic parts of who they were. When I introduced new strategies to improve focus and productivity, Jamie felt conflicted, sometimes resisting these approaches because they feared losing the parts of themself that felt unique and authentic. Jamie's journey illustrates the delicate balance between honoring one's identity and embracing growth. In such cases, it becomes vital to acknowledge and validate the client's experience, while gently introducing the possibility that growth and change can coexist with the comfort found in their current identity.

IFS fosters the kind of integrative work that can address these challenges. Of course, integration is critical for all clients, regardless of their diagnosis. Integration means we create space for our clients, helping them to explore their own narratives, while gently guiding them toward more balanced understandings of themselves. By supporting them in recognizing the strengths and limitations associated with their diagnosis and encouraging their exploration, we help ensure the diagnosis doesn't dominate their identity. Clients can then begin to cultivate new strategies for personal growth and healing. Such an integrative approach not only honors clients' lived experiences, but also empowers them to move beyond labels and embrace a fuller sense of self.

The IFS model is particularly useful in this work because it requires us to approach our clients not through a diagnosis but through their *parts*. This reinforces the reality that multiplicity characterizes all individuals. In this respect, Walt Whitman's words remain true: *We contain multitudes.* After all, we're all made up of many experiences; none of us can be narrowed down to just one impactful moment.

The IFS focus on parts also lowers the temperature surrounding a client's belief that they must change everything about themselves to experience therapeutic relief. We all know that this type of overwhelm can paralyze treatment efforts. Every one of us tends to feel discouraged when our efforts don't seem to match our need. This is where the parts work in IFS is so useful. The work provides a rationale and a structure for pursuing treatment step by step. With IFS, we tend to the parts, and transformation takes care of itself.

For all these reasons, I was very excited to integrate IFS into my play therapy approach. Naturally, I set out to look for relevant resources to support this work. But I was surprised to find there isn't much out there. There is limited information on using IFS with children and adolescents, and virtually no information on integrating IFS into play therapy. I realized that if I wanted more information, I was going to have to start the work myself, using my experiences to start a larger conversation. So that's what I did. I brought IFS into the playroom and started to integrate IFS into my play-based work with child clients. I tracked the shifts in the responses of my clients to this new approach and its tools. What I saw convinced me of the effectiveness of IFS, particularly of its synergistic value when paired with different elements of play therapy, and of its value in working with children who have trauma in their lives.

Take Addy. She came to me as a 7-year-old struggling with intense feelings of anger and sadness after her parents' recent divorce. In our sessions, Addy would often lash out at toys or retreat into silence, overwhelmed by emotions she couldn't quite name. Using aspects of play therapy, I introduced a family of puppets, encouraging Addy to assign roles and voices to each one, and allowing her to externalize and interact with the parts of herself that felt angry, scared, or alone. Using IFS language, I gently guided Addy to recognize that her "angry part" was trying to protect her "sad part," and I helped her to consider that both parts had important jobs. Over time, Addy developed compassion for these parts, and this allowed her to feel more integrated and to express her needs in healthier ways at home and school.

While IFS and play therapy work synergistically, they seem to be even more effective at addressing issues faced by members of special populations and people of color. I believe a big part of this efficacy is because the IFS approach honors and empowers all parts of an individual's internal system, which acknowledges the impact of cultural and systemic trauma while also fostering healing through self-compassion.

The approach also works incredibly well with clients dealing with trauma. When kids experience trauma or other negative life events, such as abuse, neglect, bullying, racism, violence, or educational difficulties, they may begin to hold powerful negative beliefs about themselves, such as *I'm broken*, *I'm unlovable*, or *It was my fault*. While play therapists know that children can use play to express their emotions, process their experiences, and resolve the internal conflict that can result from these beliefs, IFS therapists know that helping children explore their internal system, develop Self-to-part relationships, and unburden from these unhelpful beliefs will contribute to a more peaceful internal system. When we weave play therapy interventions with parts work—the essence of IFS—we can help kids conceptualize themselves and their experiences in healthier ways.

In the material that follows, I explain my approach to play therapy, my approach to IFS, and the work I conduct at the intersection of these two models. In chapter 2, I explain the tenets and key terms of IFS. In chapter 3, I describe the IFS flow and explain how I use IFS to center Self-energy. In chapter 4, I discuss play therapy. Chapters 5, 6, and 7 are devoted discussing some of the main activities from play therapy that I use to inspire and enact the relational, Self-energetic work of IFS. These chapters help operationalize the earlier chapters, providing tools and tips you can use to reach your clients, regardless of age, experiences, or diagnoses. In these chapters, I also offer client examples to show the broad range of uses to which Playful Parts can be put. Chapter 8 concludes the book with a reminder that you can use activities already in your toolkit.

IFS has been instrumental to my continued growth as a clinical professional, and when integrated with play therapy, it becomes even greater than the sum of its parts. Together, these two approaches help to increase clients' emotional awareness and develop a deeper relationship with their true Self and protective system. They also help therapists push the concept of experiential therapy methods to another level, allowing us to see what happens when we step away from phase-oriented models and instead follow the natural flow of the client's internal system.

As dedicated advocates, we always work to implement the best models and use the most effective tools for the young people in our care. Playful Parts offers an approach that helps us to reach our clients where they are, to facilitate their creative communication, and to experience Self-led transformation. As a combinatory model and set of tools, Playful Parts is a truly integrative model, more effective at reaching and helping transform our clients than play therapy or IFS on its own.

CHAPTER 2

Foundations in Internal Family Systems

One afternoon, after a long day of seeing my young clients, I decided to go to Target to pick up some cleaning supplies. While there, I felt I needed to treat myself for putting in a solid day of work, so I picked up a drink from Starbucks and looked at the cheap seasonal items in the Bullseye's Playground. Meandering over to the cleaning supplies, I picked out what I needed. Then, I proceeded to grab some new socks for my son and a few items I decided would look nice in my living room. Then, somehow, I found myself in the toy section. While standing in front of the LEGO® section, I began to have an inner conversation:

- **Here-and-now me:** "I don't need anything from this section."

- **Teenage me:** "You can afford the LEGOs—you work, don't you?"

- **Play therapist me**: "Just say you're buying them for your work kids."

- **7-year-old me:** "OMG! These would be sooooo fun to play with Charlotte when she comes and visits the office next week!"

Next thing I know, my checkout total is $375.65, and I'm walking out of Target with four new LEGO sets, socks for my son, cleaning supplies, and two bags of random things I don't even know what I'm going to do with.

Now, stop and pause. Can you relate to anything in this experience?

The truth is: When we look in the mirror, we see ourselves as one individual, but inside each of us are the parts of our experiences and identities that make us who we are. *Each and every one of us is made up of parts.* I've just introduced you to some of my own parts—the parts that live inside of me:

- Here-and-now Carmen

- Teenage Carmen

- Play therapist Carmen

- 7-year-old Carmen

My experience at Target is a good example of the different ways our parts can express themselves. If someone were to ask me why I even bought more LEGO sets (sets I certainly don't need), I would probably respond with something like "A part of me wanted to get them for the playroom" or "A part of me knew that it would be fun for one of the kids on my caseload."

Often, our parts contradict one another or are difficult to manage in ways we may not understand. My parts at Target interacted pretty peaceably, but that's not always the case. This is where IFS can help. IFS enables us to conceptualize and work with our parts to better understand and heal ourselves. The model helps us get to know our parts and build relationships with them. This is critical because when we're better able to understand and communicate with our parts, we're better able to decrease the conflicts inside of us, increasing the harmony within our systems and enabling our essence—or our Self (what I will typically refer to as *Self-energy*)—to lead us. In the words of IFS founder, Richard Schwartz, IFS is "a loving way of relating internally (to your parts)" but also "externally (to the people in your life)." It is "a life practice" (Schwartz, 2021, p. 4).

The concept of parts has been used by a number of other therapeutic modalities. For example, in Gestalt therapy, and some forms of Jungian therapy, parts are referred to as "ego states," "schemas," "id/ego/superego," or "archetypes." In IFS, parts represent different subpersonalities or expressions of who we are. This modality was developed in the 1980s by Dr. Richard Schwartz, a licensed marriage and family therapist with a PhD in systemic family therapy. He began developing this approach as a way to help individuals better understand and work with their inner psychological systems and the various parts that make up their personality. The model has since gained recognition and popularity.

Dr. Schwartz adopted the term *parts* after his early experiences working with clients. According to Schwartz, he was simply following his clients' lead, as *parts* was the word they most frequently used to refer to themselves. For instance, when he first began to develop the foundation for IFS, he worked with a 23-year-old young woman named Quinn, whom he states, "opened my eyes and planted the seed for IFS" (Parmalee & Schwartz, 2023, p. 8). Dr. Schwartz explained that in his interactions with Quinn, she talked about a war inside of her between different parts, each with distinct voices. According to Quinn, she had no control over what they said or did (Parmalee & Schwartz, 2023).

Schwartz argues that parts make up a plural mind—they are internal entities or subpersonalities that operate autonomously, each possessing a full spectrum of emotions, thoughts, beliefs, and sensations, and each differing in appearance, age, gender, abilities, and interests. Within the internal system, they assume diverse roles and contribute to overall functioning. When they are not exiled or in conflict over the management of vulnerable parts, they play essential roles in promoting harmony, efficiency, and well-being. When acknowledged and valued, every part embodies their own unique Self-energy.

The "family system" in IFS refers to the close and interactive relationship between our parts and our Self-energy. According to Schwartz & Sweeney (2020), our internal system is one of many systems in our world:

> A *system* can be defined as any entity whose parts relate to one another in a pattern. Thus systems include everything from watches to televisions to transit systems. In addition, by this definition all biological organisms, from bacteria to whales, are systems. Human

systems include everything from an individual's personality to a nation, and both operate according to beliefs. (p. 25)

In this way, our internal system is related to the larger, external social systems of which we're all a part, including our families, our communities, and larger institutions and other societal entities. Our internal family system remains inside of us because its role is fundamentally protective. This means that the parts operate according to an order that protects us from the vulnerability and pain we've experienced throughout our lives, regardless of from where this vulnerability and pain originated.

According to IFS, all of the parts in our internal family system take on one of three roles, relating to one another according to our interactions with external systems:

- **Manager** parts
- **Firefighter** parts
- **Exile** parts

Just as with the different members of our family, each of these parts has a specific view of the world, as well as different emotions and beliefs (Schwartz & Sweezy, 2020). When the system is functioning harmoniously, all parts are welcome, all parts are seen and heard, and all parts are in relationship with each other and with our essence, or our Self-energy. When the system is *not* functioning harmoniously, our managers and—when necessary—our firefighters work constantly to not only protect our system from external stimuli but also to protect it from other internal parts.

Before we look more closely at our parts, it's important for us to recognize that all of our parts have positive intentions. Our parts develop their behaviors as *protective* responses, typically in response to early life experiences and challenges. In IFS therapy, the goal is not to reprimand or reform any part. It is instead to understand, work with, and ultimately transform these parts as required to help individuals achieve greater balance, self-compassion, and well-being. By fostering cooperation and harmony among all parts, IFS aims to allow individuals to become their own Self-led, compassionate leaders.

Managers

I know that this *parts* language may initially feel confusing, but it can help to think of the roles occupied by the parts in straightforward terms. Our manager parts are the bosses who ensure our system is running as it should. A manager's primary goal is to keep us feeling secure, and a manager does this by exerting control. Managers are also socially adaptive, helping us fit in and have a sense of value. This is why manager parts often repeat stories about how life "should" be lived, which is information they learned from our family of origin, school, culture, or community. Managers not only take on the job of assessing and adjusting our presentation to the external world, they also try to make sense of the world by creating the narratives we rely on. They typically do these things by adopting the following behaviors:

- **Planning and controlling:** Managers often plan, organize, and maintain control over an individual's thoughts, emotions, and behaviors. They aim to prevent other parts, especially exiles, from becoming overwhelmed or experiencing painful emotions.

- **Taking responsibility and enforcing perfectionism:** Managers often exhibit a strong sense of responsibility, a desire for perfection, and a need to meet high standards. They can drive individuals to overachieve and avoid mistakes.

- **Self-criticizing:** Some managers are self-critical and may engage in negative self-talk or self-blame. They might constantly monitor and judge an individual's actions and decisions.

- **Expressing caution and avoiding risk:** Managers tend to be cautious and risk-averse. They work to prevent individuals from taking risks that could lead to harm or vulnerability.

- **Controlling others:** In some cases, managers may extend their control to other people in an individual's external life, attempting to manage or manipulate their relationships and environment for the individuals' perceived benefit.

- **Managing anxiety:** Managers often attempt to keep anxiety and distress at bay. They may use coping strategies like avoidance, denial, or rationalization to maintain a sense of safety.

- **Suppressing emotions:** Some managers suppress or dissociate from their own emotions, particularly vulnerable ones. They may discourage an individual from expressing sadness, fear, or other emotions perceived as weak.

- **Thinking logically and rationally:** Managers may emphasize logical, rational thinking and problem-solving, sometimes to the detriment of emotional or intuitive aspects of the Self.

For managers seeking to protect the internal family system by maintaining control, their motto is *never again*: Never again will these parts put down their guard and allow the system to feel the same kind of pain or shame that happened in the past.

Most of us can probably call to mind the parts of us that seek control. If not, we can think to the common scenario of the adult who experienced painful rejection as a child. For this adult, a too-vigilant manager part might drive them to seek constant approval, operating under the belief that *If I stay on top of everything, I'll never be hurt like that again.*

Firefighters

Sometimes, however, manager parts cannot maintain control and cannot ensure the harmony of the internal system. This happens when an experience sparks an emotion or feeling that is hard to process. The manager may be unable to contain the other parts, or the other parts may perceive the manager as too weak. When this happens, a firefighter part rushes in to take over and save the day.

Firefighters are reactive and impulsive, attempting to extinguish the flames of emotions that can happen inside of us when our managers are not able to fulfill their duties because the emotions or other forces involved are just too big. Often, this means that firefighters swoop in to rescue us from feeling the emotional pain of difficult situations. This can result in unhelpful behaviors that we express in big and not-so-big ways. When working with children, for instance, we might see big behaviors like defiance, verbal or physical aggression, or flagrant inattention.

However, there are other, not-so-big behaviors provoked by firefighters, and these are not always easy to see. Isolation, self-harm, and other expressions that aren't outwardly extreme can be attributed to firefighters too. Firefighters also try to take us away from emotional danger in the context of the fight, flight, or freeze responses. Firefighters are less socially acceptable than managers and will do whatever it takes to get away from the pain associated with exiles, regardless of the impact on the physical body or external relationships. This is why, whereas managers work according to a motto of *never again*, firefighters work according to a motto of *when all else fails*. Under this motto, firefighters take over the manager's job in an effort to control the system, no matter the cost. They typically do so by adopting the following overlapping behaviors:

- **Distracting:** Firefighters use distraction to keep the pain and shame they sense in other parts from overwhelming the system. Distraction can look a lot of ways, but it often occupies the physical body and can manifest as binge eating, overworking, or overexercising behaviors. It can also manifest in more mundane ways, such as binge-watching television or scrolling on social media.

- **Isolating:** Firefighters are very protective and don't want others finding out about the parts of the system that hold pain and shame. To keep these parts hidden, firefighters might push others away, including friends and family, expressing a desire to be left alone.

- **Anger and aggression:** Firefighters often use anger and aggression to manage the other parts. These big behaviors often act as a diversion tactic, ensuring others' attention (including the firefighters') is on their anger rather than their pain and shame.

- **Self-harming:** Firefighters might engage in cutting behaviors or other risky behaviors to distract themselves from their internal pain or to overpower the other parts.

- **Addiction:** Like distraction and self-harm, addictive behaviors are used by firefighters to manage, and sometimes numb, the painful parts that feel too powerful in the system.

Before discussing exiles, let's take a moment to reflect on some of the manager and firefighter parts in action in a relatively harmonious system—mine! Let's call back to my experience at Target and identify some of my different parts that came online while I was there:

- **Here-and-now Carmen:** This part presented with the most Self-energy, as communicated by calm, logical thinking: "I don't need any new toys from the toy section."

- **Teenage Carmen:** This part presented as a manager in the system to protect a younger part in the system that had been told *no* many times because *we can't afford that*. This part often shows up to remind Older Me that I work hard, that I can afford things, and that I should get what I want: "You can afford the LEGOs—you work, don't you?"

- **Play therapist Carmen:** This part presented as another manager within the system. This part came online in my internal system during my process of becoming a clinical social worker and Registered Play Therapist. This manager does not want me to be lacking in any area of the play therapy profession and wants to ensure that I will have what other play therapists have in their offices. Although this part certainly looks out for me, I personally feel this part is in relationship with my teenage part and my 7-year-old part because I buy a lot of toys that I then don't actually allow children in the office to play with: "Just say you are buying them for your work kids." (I'm sure some readers can relate!)

- **7-year-old Carmen:** Now, this little one presented in her two braided ponytails and pink sneakers. She thinks everything is about her when it comes to my work as a play therapist. She believes that all the kids are coming to see her and that she has to have the best toys to host these weekly play dates: "OMG! These would be sooooo fun to play with Charlotte when she comes and visits us next week in your office!" The interesting thing about 7-year-old me is that, despite her youth, she also has protective energy. I believe this may be because she grew up as an only child, and there were not a lot of kids around her during childhood.

If we were to spend more time getting to know each of these parts, we would learn more about them. We would learn about the life experiences, both good and bad, that informed their viewpoints and personalities. We would learn to listen to their stories and make room for their feelings within us. We would work to foster their cooperation with one another and the harmony among them. We might even get to know some of the exiles that these parts occasionally work to protect. As all of these parts are allowed to express their full selves, in all their complicated glory, they relax into making more space for the Self-energy that is so necessary to transformation.

Exiles

In some ways, our internal system is only as harmonious as the relationships its manager and firefighter parts hold with its exiles. I know that *exile* is an extreme word. And also, we use it for a reason. Our exiles are the parts of us that hold hurt, abandonment, abuse, and emotional pain. Our exiles are the parts of us that bear the deepest scars from difficult life events. At the same time, our exile parts are also our most sensitive, innocent parts.

Our managers and firefighters work to shut away our exile parts, both to protect the system and to protect exiles from their own emotions, memories, beliefs, and sensations, which threaten to overwhelm the system. Consequently, however, exiles are continually rejected, devalued, marginalized, and subject to re-traumatization. They're protected but are also pushed away by the protective system.

When an exile part is activated, the protective system has to be bigger than the exile to cover over and push away the emotions the exile brings to the forefront. This can look like a child being fearful of going to school due to being bullied by another student. The exile is the bullied part, and the protector is the part that gets into trouble on the bus so that the child must go directly to the principal's office once the bus arrives at school, instead of getting breakfast in the cafeteria, where most of the bullying happens.

Other models and methods know exile parts by other names. In fact, they're most familiar to us as "trauma." While we often distinguish between "big T" versus "little t" trauma, when viewed through the IFS lens, trauma is a unified term describing the *impact* of burdens, not the inputs. In other words, trauma does not pertain to the event that happens to us but to how we respond to that event. As IFS therapists, we understand trauma as an emotional response to an event that threatens, causes harm, and increases negative emotions. What causes this response can provide some explanatory power, but the cause is not our point of focus.

While managers and firefighters take on their roles as a consequence of the needs of the exiles, parts become exiled based on their experiences and the beliefs they come to hold about themselves, including:

- Neglect
- Attachment injuries
- Humiliation
- Boundary violations
- Hostility
- Rejection
- Criticism
- Shame

In addition, our exile parts often share common traits, such as:

- Dependence
- Spontaneity
- Openness
- Fear
- Shame
- Sadness
- Frozenness
- Fragility
- Sense of being unlovable
- Sense of abandonment
- Anger
- Powerlessness

- Sensitivity
- Emptiness
- Hopelessness

- Worthlessness
- Pain and hurt

However, all of our parts, whether managers, firefighters, or exiles, can be expressed in these and in many other ways. Our parts are always developing and can appear—or *come online*—at any time as we grow, through:

- Thoughts
- Feelings
- Sensations
- Memories
- Inner voices

- Words
- Images
- Dreams
- Physical systems
- Felt sense

Unsurprisingly, the exile's motto is *don't forget about me*, and when they become activated by interactions with other parts or with external systems, they flood us with pain, shame, and fear. We may even impair our ability to function in the here and now due to the strength of their strong feelings of vulnerability, weakness, sadness, and shame, and the corollary inability of our manager parts to manage or our firefighters to fight these feelings.

Burdens

When talking about the different protector roles played by our parts, we must discuss burdens. Burdens are negative beliefs, emotions, sensations, or other energies that are brought on by past or still-active trauma experiences. Burdens can also be passed down from generation to generation. No matter how they manifest, burdens held by the exiled parts are typically the cause of, or at the root of, imbalances within the internal system.

Although the biggest burdens are typically carried by exiles, burdens do not belong only to exiles—all of our parts can carry burdens. This is why an important goal of IFS work, particularly our work with different parts, is to help our clients identify the burdens carried by their different parts so as to support their understanding that they are not the same thing as their burdens. In fact, a client's parts are also not the same as their burdens. Their different parts *carry* the burdens associated with their negative experiences, such as attachment disruptions, neglect, and physical, sexual, and emotional abuse. We must first help clients identify these burdens before we can support them in their work to help their parts lay those burdens down.

It is true, however, that our exiles typically carry the internal system's most painful burdens, and depending on a number of variables, we may not be able to help our clients' parts unburden themselves. For instance, depending on the age of the client at the time of the trauma that produced the burdens, the beliefs associated with these burdens may have been very closely held for a very long period of time. In these and other cases, a client's burdens can become closely associated with the client, with their world, or with the stories they told (or continue to tell) themselves to help them make sense of themself and their world. Further, when a client's exile parts carry burdens while the client remains in a traumatizing environment, the difficulties associated with their burdens are compounded. This is especially the case when the client is a child. For these clients, their exiles become more entrenched and more difficult to heal. The goal of therapy in these cases is not always to unburden the parts, but to allow their parts opportunities for expression and to help their parts avoid adopting negative beliefs over the long term.

Self-Energy and the Goal of IFS

IFS aims to foster cooperation and harmony among all parts, allowing individuals to become their own Self-led, compassionate leaders. The model achieves this aim by decreasing the system's efforts to maintain control over particular parts holding particular burdens. When we can relax these efforts, we can enable the system to increase Self-energy. In IFS, the Self is, essentially, the essence of our spirit. The secure attachment between the Self and the parts is a deeply protective and reparative resource. Supporting this secure attachment is the ultimate goal of IFS. It's what stimulates the cooperation and harmony that maintains our internal balance.

Before we talk a bit more about the Self and Self-energy, let's take a deep breath. The concept of Self may be a challenge for some. It certainly was for me! When I was first trained in the model, I had a hard time grasping the whole "Self" concept. But the Self, or what I've already indicated I refer to as *Self-energy*, is not so complicated. As I've already described, it's the essence of our spirit. It consists of the positive qualities that we each possess simply by virtue of being born. It's an internal compass that helps orient our unique selves in our world.

Yes, sometimes our life experiences make our Self-energy difficulty to access or even detect. This is because when our system is not harmonious, our parts do not make space for Self-energy—or our parts may be blended (which we'll talk about in the sections that follow)—in an attempt to control the system. Consequently, our Self-energy cannot always act as the guide we need. Even so, Self-energy is an ever-present, unchanging aspect of each and every one of us, and with the right tools, we can access it and welcome its transformative presence.

IFS understands our Self-energy as expressed through the 8 Cs:

- **Calmness**
- **Curiosity**
- **Compassion**
- **Confidence**
- **Courage**
- **Clarity**
- **Connectedness**
- **Creativity**

Fig. 2.1: Focus on Feeling® 8 Cs of Self-Leadership

We can best activate our Self-energy by expressing the 8 Cs toward and through all of our parts. This is why we spend most of our time in IFS getting to know our plural mind (Schwartz & Sweeney, 2020). We conceptualize our parts by learning about their informing experiences, expressive personalities, and ways of being. As we see and hear all of our parts, accepting them for what they are, we establish relationships between and among our parts. These relationships are informed by our Self-energy and its expression through the 8 Cs: The more calmness, curiosity, compassion, confidence, courage, clarity, connectedness, and creativity we are able to express through our parts, the more Self-energy guides them. The system becomes more harmonious with less effort, fostering a virtuous circle of transformation.

Therefore, in IFS, we learn how systems work and how the parts of the system come together to function as a balanced whole. When we understand our internal system, we can begin to have a better understanding of our parts and how our parts interact with each other to protect us. We can also learn how to lead our parts to become Self-led. Again, this was a hard concept for me at the start of my IFS journey. I listened to my trainers and others with a strong history in the model claiming a goal of being "in Self," and I couldn't really understand what this meant. It seemed difficult to conceptualize an internal system in Self when the parts and their burdens are typically always present. This is why I like using the concept of being *Self-led*. This, I believe, is more attainable to me, and allows for the parts to be present though not in full control.

Fig. 2.2: The Virtuous Circle of IFS

Blended and Unblending

According to Schwartz and Sweezy (2020), the term *blending* refers to a common scenario in which parts take over, partially or completely, a person's Self. Depending on the degree of blending, the Self can remain present with some blending or be obscured completely with full blending. In other words, blending results when a person becomes so fused or merged with a particular part of their internal system that they lose their sense of Self and start to identify with the characteristics, emotions, or behaviors of that part. It's as if they become one with the part, and the part's perspective and qualities dominate their experience and decision-making. The person starts to see the world through the lens of that part and their beliefs, which are usually strongly informed by their burdens.

Blending often occurs when an individual is overwhelmed by the burdens, emotions, or behaviors associated with a particular part. For example, if a client's managerial inner critic part is very active and self-critical, the client may become blended with it and start to think and feel as though they are inherently flawed or worthless. This can be distressing and often limits their ability to access other, more adaptive parts of themselves.

In IFS, we seek to help clients unblend from their parts and to gain the distance from their parts that will enable them to see their parts with a clearer sense of those parts' roles and intentions. This distance creates space in which Self-energy can flourish, leading to self-compassion, self-leadership, and self-awareness. The unblending process is fundamental to IFS because it also enables clients to access other, more positive and adaptive parts of themselves, which can promote further healing and personal growth. I will describe its typical steps and offer an example of those steps in action. This helps to illustrate the concept of unblending and shows how important it is to the work of IFS.

STEPS TO UNBLENDING

1. **Notice the blending:** Pay attention to any shifts in the client's emotions, body sensations, or thoughts that feel overwhelming or intense. Acknowledge that this is likely a part taking over (blending). An example of this might be "I notice you're feeling a lot of anxiety right now. Can we get curious about this part that's showing up?"

2. **Name and acknowledge the part:** Help the client name the part or describe how it feels. Simply naming the part begins to create some

separation. An example of this might be "Can you sense where this anxious part shows up in your body?"

3. **Invite the part to give space:** Ask the part if it's willing to step back or give the client a little space. Emphasize that this isn't about rejecting the part, just giving it a chance to be witnessed. An example of this might be "Would this part be willing to step to the side so we can get to know it better?"

4. **Check for Self-energy:** Ask the client how they feel toward the part. If they respond with curiosity, compassion, or calm (or any other of the 8 Cs), this indicates Self-energy is present. If not, another part may be present, and unblending may need to happen at a deeper level. An example of this might be "How do you feel toward this anxious part?" If the answer is judgmental or resistant, another part might need attention first.

5. **Appreciate the part's role:** Thank the part for its efforts, even if it's causing distress. This helps reduce resistance and increases the likelihood of cooperation. An example of this might be "Thank you for working so hard to protect [*client's name*]. I see how much you care."

6. **Engage in dialogue with the part:** Once the part unblends, the Self can engage directly with it to understand the part's role, fears, and desires. An example might be "What would this part like you to know about why it's here?"

7. **Reassure the part:** Let the part know that unblending doesn't mean losing connection. It can remain close but without overwhelming the Self. An example might look like "You can stay nearby if you'd like. We just want to get to know you from some distance."

8. **Monitor and rebalance:** Throughout the session, continue to check for blending. If a part begins to take over, gently repeat the process.

By consistently practicing unblending with clients, clients learn to unblend from parts on their own. They also develop greater access to Self-energy, leading to healing and balance in their internal system.

IFS and Children

In my work, I've learned that IFS can be especially beneficial for children. This may be because the model allows us to work with kids to develop an understanding of their protective system and the role that this system plays in their big behaviors. Importantly, its tools help kids develop relationships with their parts by grasping the *why* behind the behaviors. As kids learn to listen to and understand the parts responsible for the behaviors they do not like, they also make space for the Self-energy that fosters harmony within their internal system.

All of this is wonderful, but what I love most about using IFS with kids and adolescents is that it helps us target the negative beliefs—the burdens— taken on by the child's parts. Through IFS, we learn to hear those negative beliefs and understand their *why*, and then we learn to replace them with positive, Self-energetic beliefs. This is the key to the model's lasting and transformative potential for kids, who are so often prone to identifying with their parts and with their parts' burdens.

It's important to note, however, that when I refer to "big behaviors," I do not necessarily mean "extreme behaviors." Too often, when it comes to working with kids, parents and therapists look at extreme external behaviors and overlook internal behaviors or the external behaviors that aren't quite so extreme. Take the example of a child who gets angry and aggressive at school when approached by bullies but becomes nervous and quiet in the classroom. Parents and therapists may (rightly) look to defuse the anger and aggression, but at the same time, they may fail to realize that the anxiety and withdrawal in the classroom serve a similar protective function, enabling the child to hide away their embarrassment or confusion over not understanding the lesson.

Typically, IFS can help in this scenario too, supporting families by helping children increase their emotional literacy, gain a deeper understanding of who they are in their various environments, and increase communication and connection with external elements such as family, friends, and the community.

The 5 Ps and Applying IFS

In IFS, we frequently speak of "lending our Self-energy" to our client. This is often necessary because the Self-energy of our clients can be obscured by the burdens of other parts. While IFS therapists can use the 8 Cs to communicate their Self-energy to their clients, they can also express their Self-energy to clients through the 5 Ps: presence, patience, persistence, playfulness, and perspective. These qualities, like the 8 Cs, support effective, compassionate, and healing therapeutic relationships. They ensure the IFS therapist applies IFS in the service of fostering a supportive flow:

- **Presence:** Means being fully attuned and engaged with the client in the moment. Presence involves listening deeply, withholding judgment, and offering undivided attention. It signals to clients that they are seen, heard, and valued, which fosters trust and safety.

- **Patience:** Means trusting the client's process and timeline for healing without rushing or forcing outcomes. Patience allows for the unfolding of deep emotions and parts work at a natural pace, respecting the client's readiness to explore vulnerable areas.

- **Persistence:** Means remaining steady and committed to the therapeutic process, even when progress feels slow or resistance arises. Persistence reflects the therapist's dedication to helping clients work through challenging emotions or stuck patterns with consistent support.

- **Playfulness:** Means bringing lightness, humor, and creativity into the therapeutic space. Playfulness helps disarm defenses, reduce fear, and create a sense of openness. It can invite clients to view their inner experiences from a new, less intimidating perspective.

- **Perspective:** Means holding a broad, compassionate view of the client's system and experiences. It helps the therapist see beyond immediate problems, recognizing the larger patterns and inherent potential for healing. Perspective supports the client in reframing difficult experiences and fostering hope.

By embodying the 5 Ps, therapists create an environment where clients feel supported, empowered, and encouraged to engage in the transformative process of internal healing.

With a strong foundation of 5 Ps, we can turn to the three main approaches to bringing IFS into our work: insight, direct access, and externalization. *Insight*, or in-sight, is the most common approach to using IFS therapy in session, and we typically know it as parts language. An insight approach can be fairly easy to use with adults and older adolescents who grasp the concept of parts and for whom suggestions to "ask that part of you" or "put your focus on that part" are clear and comprehensible. This approach gives the client an opportunity to focus internally and to invite a conversation between their parts and their Self.

When working with younger children, however, we tend to use *direct access*. When using direct access, we do not ask the client to relate their Self to their part; instead, we give the client our Self-energy and use that to relate to the client's part, as in the following:

> **ME:** It seems like you had a really bad day at school.
>
> **CLIENT:** I did have a bad day, and I really hate school.
>
> **ME:** I would love to know more about your hate for school. Is it okay if you tell me more?
>
> **CLIENT:** Yes, it's okay for me to talk about it.

Direct access typically works well for young children who may or may not grasp the concept of parts but who are able to answer questions about their experience of feeling a feeling, as outlined in the previous example conversation.

Finally, *externalization* refers to the process of separating or personifying parts by giving them identities, voices, and roles outside of the client's inner world through objects or drawings. This technique helps clients view their inner experiences as distinct parts rather than as integral aspects of their identity. Externalization can also be used as a method for unblending. For instance, I may ask a client to draw the "worried part" that tries to keep them safe. They then respond by drawing an army man. The drawing is an externalization of their anxiety and an identification of it as but one part of their system. Like insight and direct access, externalization of parts allows clients to:

- **Gain distance and compassion:** They learn to see the part as separate, reducing shame or overwhelm.

- **Dialogue with the part:** They can engage in a conversation with their parts, learning their intentions and building a cooperative relationship.

- **Unburden and heal:** They can work toward a goal of healing their wounded parts (exiles) and releasing their protectors from extreme roles.

Remember that IFS emphasizes that all parts are valuable and serve a purpose, even if their methods are problematic. Externalization, like insight and direct access, allows for curiosity, understanding, and eventual integration, leading to greater internal harmony in a creative way.

Case Conceptualization

When I began to use IFS in the playroom, I started to work with and understand my clients in new and different ways. Mason, an early client, stands out. I provided care for Mason after he experienced several years of verbal, physical, and emotional abuse from his parents. He preferred to engage with the toys in my playroom, especially the sandtray. As he played, we used the IFS model to help him understand his different parts and to begin to build connections to them. The results of this work shed important light on Mason's experience that helped him begin to access and lead with his Self-energy and its 8 Cs.

As I began to get to know Mason, I saw that he often expressed himself through a manager part. We came to know this part as his "big-man part." It was informed by his father, who sometimes referred to Mason as "big man." The term of endearment let Mason's system know that he was connected to his father. Not surprisingly, Mason often presented as his big-man part in order to maintain a connection with his father and decrease conflict and the risk of physical, verbal, and emotional abuse. When Mason expressed himself as big man, his behavior appeared to be strong and helpful. That's because he was being directed from the part of himself that attempted to minimize conflict. At the same time, when Mason presented as big man, it kept him from expressing his true feelings. Operating under the manager's motto of *never again*, Mason's big-man part communicated that never again would Mason experience the emotional effects of being physically, emotionally, and verbally abused.

However, sometimes, Mason's big-man manager failed. When, for example, his parents would have physical altercations, and Mason had no control of the situation, his fears started to increase. Consequently, while at home, he tended to become dissociative and reported escaping into his own inner world, which felt safer in that moment than his outer world. At school, according to his parents, Mason's protectors manifested differently. During class, when his teacher called on him when he didn't know the answer, Mason often responded with verbal aggression from his firefighter parts. This was his attempt to protect his parts, particularly his embarrassed exile, from coming to the surface and being seen by his teacher and classmates.

Early on, I knew Mason would benefit from understanding that even though his firefighter parts were behaving in difficult ways, they were trying to help him. Rather than rely on insight, I used the direct access approach, lending Mason my own Self-energy by expressing curiosity and compassion toward the protector parts that were working hard to protect him. I knew that if Mason could begin to offer his protectors curiosity and compassion, it might allow them to become less reactive or more effective in their approach to soothing his pain.

As we began to work with his parts, Mason revealed another protector part. This part sought to protect an exile: the part of Mason that had been verbally abused in radical ways. Sometimes, this protector showed up within the home setting and became the caregiver of Mason's parents in order to prevent verbal abuse. But this caregiving protector was not always successful, and sometimes Mason's exile became activated because of his parents' words and actions. When the exile made attempts to overtake the system with fears and emotions, Mason's suicidal firefighter sometimes came online, suggesting to Mason that if he were no longer alive, then he would no longer have to experience confusion and hurt by his parents.

IFS helped me understand that due to Mason's environmental experiences and his parents' behaviors, Mason's parts had taken on the burden that he was a worthless kid. I knew that we needed to focus on his protective system in order to provide him with support and care. Consequently, I supplemented my use of direct access with efforts to help him externalize his different parts. I did so by inviting Mason to represent his big man and other parts in the sandtray so that he could show and tell me about their experiences.

During our first sandtray session, I invited Mason's protective part, the big man, to the sandtray, speaking directly to him with the intention of building trust and connection: "I bet there are a lot of things you would like to say, and I would love to get to know you more. Would that be okay?" Mason responded with a yes. After receiving this confirmation, I then asked, "I'm curious how you would look if you were standing in this sandtray. What miniature would best represent you?"

Mason took his time looking at different miniatures in the room and then put several soldiers in the sandtray, spending time arranging them in a formation, with one solider leading. I asked Mason to share whatever felt right to say in the moment. He sat for a few minutes and then explained that the lead solider represented big man. He further shared that big man keeps him from crying or showing that he is scared or sad, and he leads the others to protect the ones that cannot protect themselves. I offered Mason the opportunity to talk about the other soldiers in the tray, too, helping him gain a better understanding of how his protectors helped him daily in school and at home.

Once Mason was able to represent these experiences, he became more comfortable and his protector parts relaxed, so much so that he was able to represent his exile in a sandtray with a little person figure that was smaller than all the others in the sandtray. This was a very tender moment with Mason because he desperately needed an opportunity to share this little one's experiences. Over several sessions, Mason built sandtrays focused on the little person and was able to tell me about some of his experiences with his parents. When Mason felt that he shared enough about those experiences, we looked at pictures of his sandtray and had the following conversation:

> **ME:** Let's take a few moments to look at these sandtrays and remember the experiences you shared from little you.

> **MASON:** Okay, little me is feeling a little nervous about all that I shared.

> **ME:** It's okay to feel nervous, and you can say anything you want to say about that nervous feeling, or we can build another tray.

> **MASON:** I feel a funny feeling in my tummy.

> **ME:** Put your hand on your tummy and tell it thank you for sharing all it shared.

> **MASON:** [*closes eyes, puts hands on his tummy and has a quiet moment, then smiles*]

> **ME:** How was that?

> **MASON:** It went away.

> **ME:** Is it okay to focus back on the pictures of your trays now that the nervousness gave you some space?

> **MASON:** Yes, ma'am.

> **ME:** Mason, what do you hear yourself saying when you look at those pictures?

> **MASON:** I hear a voice that sounds like my dad saying, "You are a worthless kid."

> **ME:** How often do you believe that?

MASON: Sometimes.

ME: Let's focus on the times you don't believe that. What do you hear yourself saying to yourself at those times?

MASON: That I'm a wonderful, cute, and fun kid.

ME: Let's focus on that for a bit.

MASON: Okay.

ME: Can we give up that thought of you being a worthless kid?

MASON: I would love to!

It may be surprising, but when kids start to understand that they are different from their burdens, and that they can release those burdens too, they are able to shift their perspective to more positive views of themselves, which can result in a shift in their behaviors.

Conclusion

According to Schwartz and Sweezy (2020), "When we help our distracting parts relax and our exiles unburden, all the activity and noise inside drops off and we have access to the courage and clarity of the Self, which shifts our perspective" (p. 54). In my work with children like Mason, I have been able to see shifts in the child's view of their system and themselves as a whole. I have also seen that this new perspective can impact external behaviors in sometimes critical ways. When children experience their own Self-energy, they strengthen their capacity for its 8 Cs and become more capable of self-transformation.

CHAPTER 3

Parts and Flow

Thirteen-year-old Bronwyn was brought to therapy by her parents because she was bullied at school and displaying withdrawal behaviors from friends and family. Her parents were even more concerned because they found out that Bronwyn had been cutting herself on her inner thigh. After completing a traditional psychological assessment and conducting a parent meeting, I had my first IFS session with Bronwyn. I am—as are most child therapists—very familiar with big behaviors like cutting because they are the ones that drive families to seek therapy for their children. Behaviors such as defiance and acting out—or, as with Bronwyn, withdrawal and cutting—alarm loved ones, leading them to take action and seek therapy. Parents or caregivers who bring their children to therapy for big behaviors like these usually assume that the therapist will help put a stop to the behaviors that are disrupting the family.

However, as you likely inferred from the previous chapter, the IFS model doesn't target behaviors, nor does it make behavior modification its goal. Its power is not just in the 8 Cs and 5 Ps through which Self-energy can be fostered, nor is it just in the insight, direct access, and externalization through which unburdening can occur. It is also in its *flow*, or the iterative steps that enable therapists to work with clients to unburden their parts and establish new relationships that support an integrated and balanced internal system. By inviting in the Self and its healing energy, these new relationships open space for new behaviors sustained by calmness, curiosity, compassion, confidence, courage, clarity, connectedness, and creativity. Over time, these qualities, the 8 Cs, foster new ways of being that make the behaviors often described as "big," unnecessary.

During our first session, Bronwyn explained she was being bullied by a group of mean girls at school. She said that when they talked about her, she felt like she was 5 years old, on the first day of kindergarten, and full of fears and tears. Bronwyn said she was picked on in kindergarten because she often cried. She shared that she always tried her best now to not cry at school because she didn't want to be called a crybaby.

When I asked Bronwyn what she did instead of crying, she shared that some days she tried to find a place to be alone, and other days she went to the bathroom and cut herself. She explained that when being alone didn't make her feel better, she turned to the cutting behaviors so that she could feel in control again.

I used the IFS model, especially insight work, to talk to Bronwyn and explain that what she was describing suggested that there were two protectors inside of her that were helping to keep her little 5-year-old part from showing up at school. The first protector was a manager doing its best to control the situation by making sure that Bronwyn went away from others when she had the urge to cry. When that didn't work and her 5-year-old part got too close to making an appearance, Bronwyn's second protector—a firefighter—swooped in to distract this 5-year-old by any means necessary. In Bronwyn's case, this meant engaging in self-harming behaviors. Bronwyn said that she felt like she understood this, and she agreed that she engaged in cutting behaviors as a way to stay safe and not cry at school.

The truth is, we're all a little like Bronwyn. We're all made up of different parts that work to maintain our internal system's equilibrium. As I explained in the previous chapter, some of these parts take on managerial responsibilities, but if these managers struggle, then our firefighter parts step in to ensure that our internal system continues to work. Both manager and firefighter parts seek to contain and protect our exiles—the parts of us that our protectors believe need to stay hidden away to ensure our internal system keeps working. Yet their methods sometimes contribute to behaviors that maintain an imbalanced internal system, even if the imbalance helps our exiles stay hidden or "safe."

Usually, our parts' methods are informed by the burdens they carry as a consequence of the big and small traumas that we've all—every one of us—experienced. The parts with the biggest burdens can exert unequal influence in our system, causing imbalances and closing off parts from the Self-energy that we otherwise possess. As I pointed out in the previous chapter, burdens weigh on parts as beliefs. These aren't explicit or conscious beliefs (although they can be); they're typically implicit, unconscious beliefs—beliefs we don't even realize we have. This is one reason that IFS methods like insight, direct access, and externalization are so useful.

Our burdened parts adopt a variety of behaviors as a result of these beliefs. Importantly—and maybe surprisingly—some of these behaviors look healthy, like setting an alarm every day to wake up on time or ensuring that we pay our bills every month. Other behaviors look unhealthy, like drinking too much or, as with Bronwyn, harming ourselves. Sometimes, we seek out therapy, or our loved ones do, when our behaviors push us in challenging directions. When Bronwyn started to withdraw at school and engage in self-harm behaviors, for instance, her parents sought intervention.

Because the IFS model encourages therapists to consider that all behaviors are evidence that our parts are working to safeguard our system, we approach behaviors, even those needing intervention, as essentially protective. As with Bronwyn, we know that they're initiated by managers and firefighters trying to protect the system from being flooded by an exile's traumas. Their protective intent does *not* mean that protective behaviors can't be dangerous and have terrible consequences. They absolutely can. But, from a therapeutic perspective, even simply approaching behaviors that are frightening or that have potentially lethal consequences *as also serving a protective function* can enable an individual to access their Self-energy and activate the 8 Cs. The IFS flow offers this approach. Remember Schwartz's

(2020) words: There are no bad parts. There are no bad behaviors either. For Bronwyn and others, big behaviors are simply the behaviors that are most effective at shielding exiles from exposure.

Of course, without Self-led intervention, this type of sustained protection requires ongoing pain (Schwartz, 2023). A lot more importantly, if not quite as obviously, it keeps us from self-expression. For example, when Bronwyn would withdraw or self-harm, her manager and firefighter parts took over her system, limiting the space available for her Self-energy and preventing her Self from leading. This limitation is the result of overburdened parts: They interfere with self-expression, rigorously maintaining an imbalanced internal system that keeps us from experiencing the healing Self. As long as Bronwyn's manager and firefighters continued to exert undue influence, her essence— that which makes Bronwyn her own unique Self—would stay obscured.

Therefore, my IFS-informed goal for Bronwyn was not to stop her from withdrawing from her friends and family or from cutting. My goal was to support her in unburdening her parts so that she could begin to experience the Self-energy that could help her experience a more harmonious internal system. My goal was to involve her in the flow of IFS. When parts, especially exiles, are able to put down their burdens and make room for the Self, the behaviors they've adopted to ensure their sense of safety can naturally stop.

IFS Flow

The flow of IFS is guided by efforts to:

- Achieve balance and harmony in the system

- Create loving relationships with all parts

- Differentiate parts from Self-energy

- Unburden negative beliefs about the Self and free parts from extreme roles

- Acquire the ability to lead with Self-energy

- Translate changes and shifts in the internal system to external relationships

Again, the flow of IFS is iterative. This means that achieving sustained balance and harmony in the system is both the beginning and the end of our work. We first initiate IFS by identifying parts of the system, then by working with clients to differentiate the parts from one another and from the Self. This is the work of unblending, described in the previous chapter. Through unblending, we identify all the different parts that make up the internal system. With Bronwyn, identifying the different parts of her and starting the unblending process was at work from our very first conversations, in which I introduced the concept of her internal system and its protective parts.

We then work to bring these parts into loving relationships with one another by spending time getting to know them and getting them to know one another. This requires taking the time to listen to the protectors and find out why they do the job they do. It also requires learning what the protectors are protecting.

Next, we continue the work of differentiation through unblending. As our parts become differentiated, they can begin to share more information about their burdens and experiences. Continued work with the parts will eventually lead to unburdening, which allows each part to release the negative beliefs it's holding. Once released, positive beliefs can be brought into the system instead.

When the parts are freed, the Self can lead, and the internal system can achieve a balance that can influence external relationships. This means that when clients like Bronwyn release the negative beliefs they're holding about themselves, and begin to lead with Self-energy and the 8 Cs, they are free to stop the behaviors that once sustained those beliefs and the burdens informing them because that heightened level of protection is now understood to be unnecessary.

IFS Steps

While IFS is iterative, its flow is typically initiated through fluid, therapist-supported steps:

1. Identify a protective part and focus in on it.

2. Unblend the part from the Self, welcoming in Self-energy.

3. Develop a Self-to-part relationship.

4. Address fears and concerns of protective parts and offer hope for the exile.

5. Hear the story of the exiled part.

6. Unburden the part.

7. Bring in positive qualities.

The overview is divided into two categories of work. The first four steps focus on understanding the protective system, specifically the managers and firefighters, by fostering trust and building a relationship with these parts. The sixth and seventh steps are more explicitly healing. We operationalize these steps through the 6 Fs, a flexible process designed to guide clients in identifying and unblending their parts while encouraging connection and collaboration among them. Despite the enumerated list that follows, which I know suggests a regimented-process approach, the 6 Fs is anything but. The list should be understood as descriptive rather than prescriptive, allowing for flexibility in meeting each client's unique experience.

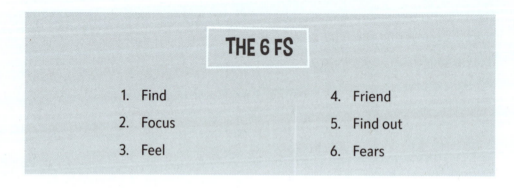

THE 6 FS

1. Find	4. Friend
2. Focus	5. Find out
3. Feel	6. Fears

The 6 Fs are designed to help us identify all of a client's protective parts and, later, to meet the exiles that these parts are protecting. The work can be operationalized in different ways. For some clients, the 6 Fs can be used as the basis for interviewing each part. For other clients, sequencing the 6 Fs through interviews or other techniques might not be as effective. These clients might need to spend a lot of time on finding their parts or focusing on them before they can identify how they feel toward any one part. Or they may need to better understand their part's fears before they can start developing a relationship with it.

Sometimes, however, clients are comfortable finding out more about a part but are uncomfortable or unable to discuss a part's fears. This is why we proceed according to the direction indicated by our client's internal system. Only when their parts feel deeply understood will they be able to share their fears and move toward healing the exile. This can take an indeterminate amount of time. To get a feel for how long, let's take a closer look and learn more about how to implement the 6 Fs in IFS work.

Find and Focus

Some clients, particularly young adults or adults, experience the work of locating and possibly even understanding their parts to be pretty easy. These clients may already have a sense that a younger version of themselves lives inside of them. They may, for instance, be accustomed to acknowledging that they have an inner child within them who has feelings and needs of its own. They may not have considered their inner child as a fully embodied part, with specific sensations and feelings, and with its own burdens, but they may find it easy to conceptualize. Clients who are comfortable with the concept of their inner child are likely also comfortable expressing curiosity about this part's impact on the internal system.

Other clients, however, adults and children alike, don't understand their parts in this way. This is so common because many of us tend to cope with traumas by severing the connection between our mind and body. Without this relationship, it can be a struggle for our minds to tune into our physical sensations, or to find where in the body those sensations are located. This is the case even for clients who understand the concept of parts and who grasp the general importance of identifying and unblending their parts from one another.

As IFS therapists, our supportive guidance in helping clients find and focus on their parts, and understand them as embodied, is critical. To support this work, we can ask our clients to notice their physical sensations when certain topics of conversations come up. We can ask them to consider what images they return to again and again. We can ask them what they feel physically when they're around certain people or what kinds of thoughts they think:

- What do you feel in your body right now?

- What are you noticing?

- Where do you notice that in your body?

- What does that feel like? Look like? Sound like?

For clients who struggle to answer these questions, and particularly for young clients, I frequently refer to cultural touchstones like the movie *Inside Out*. I'll ask my client if they've seen the movie, and I play the part of the movie in which the main character's emotions are introduced. I then ask my client about *their* different emotions—how they are feeling in session and how they know that they are feeling those feelings.

When clients find and name a feeling or an emotion, we then focus on it. When, for instance, Bronwyn identified an emotion such as anger, I followed up with questions like:

- What does it feel like?

- Where does it feel like that?

- Does it seem like it stands alone, or does it feel like it is being held?

- What does it look like?

- What does it sound like?

I supplement these questions with activities, such as mapping or sandtray, which I discuss in the chapters that follow. However, any activities that help provoke and channel a client's curiosity toward finding and focusing on their parts as embodied are useful.

Activities such as these also help therapists more capably navigate repeated responses of "I don't know." If my experience is any indication, every therapist—especially therapists who work with kids—hear "I don't know" at least once every session. This phrase can be endlessly frustrating to parents, but in IFS, we know that "I don't know" are a protector's words.

The truth is, our clients often *don't* know: Protectors take on attitudes and behaviors that ensure the exile parts remain hidden away, where they can be protected from and also exert power over the internal system and the Self. Powerful parts in our client's internal system have a vested interest in keeping our client in the dark as a method of protection. That's why I often ask my client to tell me what they *do* know, or I ask if there are fears or confusion connected to their "I don't know."

While we want to make room for "I don't know" to function as protective, we also want to make room for the possibility that it is an expression of neutrality. In session, kids may not know, may not be sure, or just may not care. Luckily, the time and activities we spend finding and focusing on their different parts help our clients practice expressing curiosity, which moves them beyond "I don't know" and helps them to go further into the 6 Fs. This is necessary because once clients are able to approach their parts as embodied, they can begin to consider why the part is located where it's located, why it expresses what it expresses, and what memories it holds onto.

Let's take a look how finding and focusing worked with Bronwyn. We approached the work using the context of a home situation because she had recently had a big disagreement with her parents. I first invited Bronwyn to put her attention on this event and to start to notice what was happening in her thoughts and in her body as she put her focus there. Then, I asked what parts of her were present in that situation. I invited her to express these parts on a piece of paper with shapes or colors. In doing so, Bronwyn identified two parts of her that were present during this disagreement: anger and frustration. This helped us know the parts of her that needed the most attention during our session, which are known as *target parts*. To help her become more connected to these parts, I asked focusing questions like

"When you look at your paper, what are you noticing in your body or in your thoughts?" This gave her time and space to start to build a better awareness of each part.

Feel

The preceding questions deepen our awareness of a client's target part and help us understand how the client experiences that part. This, in turn, allows us to move closer to uncovering how the client *feels* toward that part. We start the discussion of feeling by asking clients to reflect inward as they find and focus on a particular part. Then, we simply ask our client how they feel toward the part (Schwartz & Sweezy, 2020).

Although we want to know how our client feels toward the part, we also want to know the origin of their feeling. For clients with imbalanced internal systems or overburdened parts—so, almost all of our clients—the way they feel toward their target part will tell us if that part is blended with another part (including what other part it's blended with) and how much of the client's Self is present in the target part.

A seemingly simple question such as "How do you feel toward this part?" can bring a range of feelings to the surface. Clients may feel sad, angry, or embarrassed about their part. Conversely, they may feel protective or neutral toward it, responding with a version of "I don't know." Or they may feel overwhelmed or annoyed by our questions. Typically, any feelings that are not expressed through one of the 8 Cs, or through other positive words or statements, signal the presence of another part—usually a protector part that rushes in to try to stop what it perceives as a threat to the system.

For Bronwyn, when I initially asked her how she felt toward the part of her that cuts, she stated she didn't know how she felt toward that part of her. We discussed the part a little more, and I explained that all of our parts are there to protect us in their own special way, even if the protection sometimes caused harm to ourselves or others. Bronwyn sat for a few moments with this information before stating, "For some reason, that makes sense to me— this part is trying to protect me from the big hurt with a small hurt." When I then asked her again how she was feeling toward that part that cuts, she was able to say that she had compassion for that part and wanted to know more about why it felt like it had to hurt her.

This is an ideal example of the way that uncovering feelings toward a part can lead to Self-energy. At first, Bronwyn seemed unable to feel toward her part. But her neutrality was actually an openness into which we could express curiosity. This is key to the efficacy of IFS. We support our clients as they uncover their feelings toward their different parts, enabling their parts to relate to one another. Thereby, we open a pathway to increase Self-energy and build a more balanced relationship between the Self and parts.

beFriend

Friending, or beFriending, refers to the support we offer our clients in establishing a friendly relationship with and among their parts. Again, we can only help a client befriend their parts when the client has revealed that their feelings toward their parts are in some way Self-led or that there is room in their parts for the expression of Self-energy (Anderson et al., 2017).

I typically use activities from play therapy to support my clients in connecting to and befriending their parts, and I'll discuss these more specifically in the chapters that follow. However, in the typical flow of IFS, we foster a client's relationship with their parts by supporting them in cultivating the 8 Cs toward their part. When clients can express calmness, curiosity, compassion, confidence, courage, clarity, connectedness, and creativity, they're able to deepen their relationship with their parts through connection. To support this work, I encourage the client to use their Self-energy to make meaningful contact with their parts and get to know how each part interacts within the internal system. This means asking the client questions like:

- Does it (the part) know that you're here?

- What's it starting to notice about you?

- How is it responding to you?

- Does it know who you are?

- Does it know how old you are?

Our clients' answers to these kinds of questions are critical to the work of befriending the part—not necessarily because the content of the answers is so important, but because the process of asking our parts questions and allowing our parts to answer gives them a chance to be heard and validated. This enables the beginnings of a friendship between the part and the Self because it enables our parts to learn to trust the Self and its ability to lead the system.

I initiated befriending with Bronwyn by first ensuring that she had enough Self-energy present to approach her frustrated part with curiosity and compassion. I guided her to take a few deep breaths and check in with herself to see how she felt toward that part. She expressed a sense of openness and curiosity, and I knew we were ready to begin to deepen the relationship through the work of befriending. Bronwyn kept her eyes on the shapes and colors she'd placed on the paper, and I asked if she was connected to the frustrated part. Bronwyn closed her eyes and said, "Yes, it feels like we're sitting there together." I then ask her how that part was responding to this. Bronwyn replied that it felt like the part was getting closer, like she was looking at a mirror and she and the part were smiling at each other. Bronwyn shared that although this felt "a little weird," she also felt more connected to herself.

Find Out

Finding out refers to the work of deepening the Self-to-part relationship, and it requires finding out more information about the part. Finding out more about the part gives it a chance to be seen and heard. It also gives the client a chance to continue to cultivate curiosity, compassion, and connection toward the part, especially if that part is misunderstood by or in conflict with other parts. The process of finding out invites the client to approach their inner experiences with openness, free from judgment or the desire to immediately change or fix the part. By taking more time to listen and understand, the client continues to build trust between the Self and the part, based on seeing, respecting, and valuing the part (Schwartz, 2023).

The work of finding out reflects and confirms the core belief in the IFS model that all parts have positive intentions, even if their actions create distress. Rather than viewing parts as obstacles, clients build a fundamental appreciation of their parts as protectors or holders of pain. Further, finding out more about a part can help to shift a client's stance from resistance to collaboration, which can then pave the way for deeper healing and integration. As trust grows and deepens, parts can begin to relax, enabling Self-energy to take the lead, and ultimately allowing them to release extreme roles and access the exiled part.

To facilitate finding out, I encourage my client to embody Self-energy to make meaningful contact with the part while also asking the client deeper questions about the part, such as:

- What does it (the part) want you to know?

- What is its intention for you?

- What is its job?

- How old is it?

- What would it rather be doing?

- What does it need?

Finding out, for Bronwyn, was straightforward because the Self-to-part relationship had been developed. Consequently, I invited Bronwyn to first imagine that she was hanging out in her favorite place. She shared that she was sitting on a beach with her toes in the sand. Next, I invited her to imagine that she was sitting at the beach beside her frustrated part, having a conversation. She smiled but asked, "What do I say to it?" I invited her to ask this frustrated part what it wanted her to know, and I encouraged her to listen to its reply. Bronwyn thought for a moment, then responded that frustration often comes in to help her not feel sad or scared. I invited her to ask her frustrated part if it likes always showing up, to which Bronwyn paused and then said, "No, not really. It doesn't like always showing up." I then invited her to ask what it would rather be doing, and she smiled and said, "Absolutely nothing."

Fears

Although the work to uncover a part's fears constitutes a separate step in the 6 Fs, I think of it as an extension of the preceding steps. In general, relationships aren't always straightforward and don't always allow for an easy exchange of feelings. In most of our relationships, we don't just feel the positive feelings associated with the 8 Cs—we also navigate fear, anxiety, worry, overwhelm, and other challenging emotions and feelings. In this way, *finding out* includes finding out what a part fears. Getting more comfortable identifying these fears offers clients more opportunities to build the Self-to-part relationship. However, it also gives us a chance to start to focus on what exile the protector is protecting. To this end, we ask our clients like:

- What is this part scared of?

- What does this part think might happen if they no longer did their job?

Clients typically answer these kinds of questions in a variety of ways. They may say something like, "I'm worried that another part of me will get hurt," "I don't want to lose my role," or "I'm afraid that the exile will come out."

To go further into the root of the part's fears, we respond with validation: "Your fears and concerns are important" or "What if I can help you not have to work so hard?" We also continue asking questions, prompting the protector to reflect and go deeper until they're able to give expression to all the fears motivating their answers.

During my work with Bronwyn, we addressed many of the protective parts that showed up at school and at home—especially those that showed up as a consequence of bullying. Some of Bronwyn's protective behaviors, which were motivated by fear, included avoiding group activities, feeling anxious and withdrawn around peers, and sometimes engaging in self-harm behaviors. To help Bronwyn consider this fear, I asked her a variety of questions:

> **Me:** Bronwyn, can we take a moment to notice that part of you that feels like staying away from other kids at school?

> **Bronwyn:** Yeah, okay.

> **Me:** When you put your focus on that part, where do you feel it in your body?

BRONWYN: It's in my chest . . . kind of heavy, like a weight.

ME: Let's stay with that heaviness in your chest for a moment. Just notice it without needing to change it.

BRONWYN: [*nods*] Okay . . . I'm focusing on it.

ME: If that heavy feeling had a shape or image, what might it look like?

BRONWYN: I think it's like a small gray cloud.

ME: That's helpful. Does this cloud feel like it is holding anything, maybe an emotion or a thought?

BRONWYN: Yes, it feels kind of sad and nervous.

ME: How do you feel toward this cloud?

BRONWYN: [*pauses*] I don't know . . . I guess I feel a little annoyed with it. I wish it would go away.

ME: You are annoyed by it and wish it would go away. Let's let the cloud know you feel that way but also see if we can get curious about it. Would it be okay to ask it why it's there?

BRONWYN: Yeah, I guess so.

ME: Can we let the cloud know that you're here to listen and not make it leave? Maybe ask what it needs you to know.

BRONWYN: [*quiet for a moment*] It says it's just trying to protect me. It doesn't want me to feel embarrassed or get picked on.

ME: That makes sense. Can you thank it for trying to protect you?

BRONWYN: Okay . . . I told it. I think maybe it feels a little lighter now.

ME: Can we ask the cloud what it's afraid might happen if it wasn't there to protect you?

BRONWYN: [*pauses*] It says I might get left out or picked on . . . like before at school.

ME: That's a big fear. Can we let it know you understand why it's doing this?

BRONWYN: [*pauses*] Yeah, I told it. It's not as heavy now, but I can still feel it.

ME: I wonder if we can ask the cloud what it thinks would happen if you tried talking to some classmates.

BRONWYN: It says . . . I might say something stupid, and people will think I'm weird and talk about me.

ME: That's really helpful to know. Can you let the cloud know you hear its concern? Maybe ask it if it remembers a time that happened.

BRONWYN: It remembers last year when I said something wrong in math class and some kids laughed at me and talked about it at lunch.

ME: That sounds like a tough memory. Can we let the cloud know that you're a little older now and that you'll be there to help if something like that happens again?

BRONWYN: Yeah . . . I think it feels a little less scared now. I think it just wants me to be careful.

ME: That makes sense. Let's thank it for trying to keep you safe. Would it be okay to ask if it would step back a little during class, just to see how things go?

BRONWYN: I think it's okay with that . . . it's not as heavy now.

By addressing the protector's fears, Bronwyn learned again and again that this part was trying to shield her from past embarrassment. Engaging with the part and understanding its history allowed Bronwyn to gently reassure and negotiate with it, softening its protective stance while empowering her to take small steps forward.

Shedding light on a part's fears is hard work, and it can take an extended amount of time to address. This happens because fear can be hard to talk about. This is especially true when a protector's main goal is to protect a vulnerable exile. Questions that get close to a protector part's deepest fears can cause that part to protect more strongly. In fact, it frequently causes other protector parts to appear. When this happens, we can identify the target part and then ask any other protective parts to step back so that we can continue working with the exile part that it's protecting.

Helping our clients learn about the fears held by their parts is necessary because these fears lead to their exiles. In fact, by asking all the protector parts to step back, we invite the exiles to appear. This is the point: We *want* our clients to get to know their protective parts well enough that they feel comfortable revealing the exiles. Why? Because the overburdened exile parts—our internal system's most vulnerable parts—are what manager and firefighter parts work so hard to insulate and protect. When we gain access to them, we can help to heal them, building a relationship that allows them to more comfortably lighten their load.

Unburdening Exiles

After protective parts and their feelings and fears have been identified, and after a trusting relationship has been established, the exiles appear. At this point, the client's Self can often lead the healing process, using the 8 Cs to guide their interactions.

Healing the exiles is an extension of the work of unburdening. It's also an extension of the 6 Fs: The client witnesses their part's story and offers empathy and validation, which allows the part to release the burdens it has carried, often for many years. The process often involves revisiting past experiences to retrieve exiled parts that are stuck there and to help them to understand they are no longer alone. This then frees the protectors from their extreme protective roles, which in turn allows them to take on more positive, balanced functions. As all parts heal, the client can experience greater internal harmony, resilience, and self-leadership, fostering lasting emotional and psychological well-being.

The Hope Merchant

In IFS, unburdening and healing is led by the Hope Merchant, a role enacted by the therapist or practitioner. The Hope Merchant represents the part of therapist that holds hope and belief in the client's healing process, even when the client may feel stuck or hopeless. This part reflects the therapist's confidence that all parts, no matter how extreme or burdened, can be healed and integrated into the system.

The Hope Merchant offers gentle reassurance and expresses optimism, helping the client stay engaged in the process. The Hope Merchant can also serve as a model for the client's internal system, encouraging their protective parts to trust the process and consider the possibility of healing and transformation. The Hope Merchant underscores the importance of the therapist's attunement, compassion, and unwavering belief in the client's capacity to heal, reinforcing the core IFS principle that every part has a positive intention and that the system naturally seeks balance and harmony. Acting as the Hope Merchant is an invitation from the therapist's Self to the client's protector, as well as to the client's Self, to be curious about whether the part is interested in not having to work as hard to protect the system (Schwartz & Sweezy, 2020).

The Hope Merchant's questions can serve as a transition point between the protector and the exile. That's why, in my capacity as the Hope Merchant, I ask the following:

- If we could help the part you're protecting feel better, do you think it might be open to that?

- What if we could ease your hard feelings about _____?

- Would you be open to letting us help the part you're protecting?

- Would it interest you if we could help release the shame the part you protect is carrying?

- If we could work with this part so it doesn't overwhelm you with shame, would you feel comfortable letting us connect with it?

- If we could unburden the worthlessness this part holds, would that be something you'd consider?

- Would you be interested if we could help the part feel more/less ___?

- If we could reassure the part you protect that it won't overwhelm the system, would you be willing to let us support it?

- There's a way to release all the (shame, worthlessness, etc.) if you're open to it.

- I understand it feels impossible, but if it were possible, would you want to explore it?

- If we could help the part of you that feels lonely and scared, would you still feel the need to work so hard to be perfect?

However, when we, as therapists, seek access to the exile, our clients' protectors often respond with specific fears rooted in their role of safeguarding the system. These fears often arise from a deep-seated belief that the exile's pain must remain hidden to avoid overwhelming the client (Anderson et al., 2017). Common fears include:

- **Fear of overwhelm:** The protector worries that allowing access to the exile will unleash overwhelming emotions, potentially leading to a breakdown or emotional flooding.

- **Fear of reliving original trauma:** Protectors often believe that revisiting the exile's pain will re-traumatize the client, repeating the suffering the exile originally endured.

- **Fear the client isn't strong enough:** The protector may doubt the client's capacity to handle the exile's burdens, fearing that the client lacks the resilience to process deep-seated wounds.

- **Fear of losing control:** Protectors often hold the belief that their control is the only thing keeping the system stable. Allowing access to the exile might lead to chaos or emotional instability.

- **Fear of exposure and vulnerability:** The protector may feel that the exile's pain is too raw or shameful, fearing that revealing it (even to the therapist) will leave the client vulnerable to judgment or rejection.

- **Fear the therapist won't understand or help:** Some protectors worry that the therapist will not fully grasp the exile's pain or might mishandle the process, leaving the client feeling misunderstood or invalidated.

- **Fear of permanent damage:** The protector may believe that if the exile's pain resurfaces, it could cause lasting harm to the client's psyche, potentially leading to breakdowns or long-term dysfunction.

- **Fear of the exile taking over:** The protector might fear that if the exile is given attention, it will dominate the system with overwhelming emotions, pushing out the client's sense of Self.

- **Fear of losing purpose:** Some protectors see their role as essential to the client's survival. If the exile heals, the protector might fear that it will become irrelevant or unnecessary.

- **Fear of uncertainty:** Protectors may feel that the current dynamic, though difficult, is familiar and predictable. Healing the exile introduces uncertainty, which can feel threatening.

When clients express these fears, therapists can help their protectors feel safer by:

- Acknowledging and validating the protector's fears.

- Clarifying that the protector won't be bypassed or disrespected.

- Inviting the protector to witness the process to ensure the exile's experience is handled with care.

- Pacing the work, allowing the protector to step back gradually and with consent.

This is part of the Hope Merchant's work—to continually allow protectors to express fears, fostering trust that the therapist intends to protect the entire system. By repeatedly providing this support, protectors can begin to relax and allow for deeper healing. It also lays the important foundation for unburdening and healing their system's exiles. To make this work of healing a bit more straightforward, the IFS model offers a five-step process for healing, which I discuss next:

- Witnessing

- Retrieval and Do-Over

- Unburdening

- Invitation

- Integration of Changes

Healing Exiles

WITNESSING

This is my favorite part of the process because it's the part in which we really start to understand a client's story, including what experiences informed their different parts and contributed to their imbalanced internal system. However, it's important to note that "witnessing" refers not to the therapist acting as witness but to the client's Self acting as witness. We facilitate this witnessing so that the exile can share their experience with the client's Self. The therapist supports this by modeling Self-energy through their own expression of the 8 Cs (Schwartz & Sweezy, 2020).

When we work toward enabling our client to witness an exile, we invite the exile to explain what happened to it and why it feels the way it feels. I typically use activities from play therapy to encourage witnessing, but you can also ask direct questions to solicit information from the exile:

- If you were in a movie, what would I see?

- What do you want us/me to know about you?

- Can you let me know what happened to you?

Perhaps surprisingly, exiles often want to talk and explain themselves, but not always. Older children and adults in particular may not want us — as therapists—to know their story. That is okay. When this happens, it tells us that the exile may still be protected and have fears and concerns with moving forward. We can address this by asking questions like "What are your fears or concerns with telling your story?" Once the fears and concerns have been identified and addressed, then we can move forward with witnessing.

RETRIEVAL AND DO-OVER

Exiles are typically trapped in the original time and place in which they were burdened. Retrieval and do-over refers to the act of pulling the exile away from this narrative context and bringing them into the here and now or to another internal place that feels safe. We can offer retrieval and do-over once a client has shared their exile's experience—what happened to the exile that resulted in their burdens. Once the client has given voice to their exile, the Self can extract the exile from that narrative context. Sometimes, retrieval happens before witnessing because the exile needs to be pulled out of the original scene in which it accrued its burdens in order to share its story (Schwartz & Sweezy, 2020).

Let's return to Bronwyn to illustrate this. In early sessions with Bronwyn, she shared that she didn't want to have the feelings she had when she was 5 years old in her kindergarten class. She wanted to let those go. Therefore, once she was able to establish a relationship between her Self and this 5-year-old exile, we worked to retrieve the 5-year-old from the ongoing story about her kindergarten experience by explaining that, in fact, kindergarten was over and Bronwyn was now a teenager. She didn't want or need any part of her to stay in that kindergarten class.

At this point, we offer the exile an opportunity for a do-over, meaning we give the exile what they needed from their original experience but did not receive. Sometimes, what an exile needs is satisfied by simple retrieval: For instance, an exile may have needed to be heard, to be supported, and to be advocated for. In this case, establishing a relationship with the exile, giving the exile a chance to be heard, giving the exile support, and advocating for the exile serve as both retrieval and do-over. Other times, the exile needs the original experience to be re-narrated so they can understand that in the here and now there is a real protector that can take care of them—a Self-led protector of the whole system—and not just an overburdened manager or firefighter part.

To better understand this, let's take a look at an illustrative example from a completely different client—this time, an adult. Although this book is primarily geared toward using IFS and play therapy with children, in my practice I have seen that my approach can be effective with adults as well.

In fact, adult clients can help show the importance of listening for, engaging with, and getting to know the parts in our system that carry childhood experiences. The truth is, we don't "outgrow" these parts: We take them with us.

This particular client was a 45-year-old female who had an exile that carried a burden of sexual abuse from her childhood. The exile was stuck in time, at the age of 10 to 12, carrying a heavy burden of shame. We needed to retrieve my client's exile from the old narrative of sexual abuse by using the client's Self-energy to pull the exile into the present day. By explaining to the exile that the Self was now 45 years old and in control of the internal system—control that it was able to demonstrate by engaging with the exile—the retrieval allowed the exile to feel safe enough to tell its story. It understood that it had the protection of the client in the here and now.

At this point, my client offered the exile a do-over. She explained to her 10- to 12-year-old exile that in the here and now, the exile could rely on the client's trustworthy Self to keep her safe. In this do-over, my client explained to her exile that she was now 45 years old: "I'm older and more independent than you could be when you were 10, and I'm not going to let that bad thing happen ever again."

Obviously, this requires trust between the exile and the client's Self, trust that is often a result of the 6 Fs and the resulting Self-to-part relationships. Sometimes, exiles need proof that the bad thing that happened won't ever happen again. To this end, the exile can be updated with the client's current age and with information on how the client keeps themselves safe. When the exile is retrieved, they are no longer in the space of experiencing the same trauma. The exile may benefit from reassurance on the kind of safety and protection the Self can provide.

UNBURDENING

As I pointed out in the previous chapter, much of the work of IFS has to do with unburdening various parts. However, healing depends on unburdening exiles in particular, or helping the exiles let go of the negative beliefs associated with the experiences that created its burdens (Spiegel, 2017).

Typically, these beliefs take the form of *I'm bad, I'm not worthy, I shouldn't be here, I'm unlovable,* or *I deserve to be hurt.*

In the previous example, my client's 10- to 12-year-old exile needed to let go of the belief that she acquired during her abuse—namely, that she couldn't trust other parts and yet she couldn't survive on her own. This is a burden carried by many child abuse victims, particularly those abused by a family member. If we think about it, it makes sense: As a child, they couldn't trust the people who were supposed to protect them, and yet they needed those people to survive. After retrieval and do-over, my client unburdened her exile by continuing to explain to her that in the here and now, her other parts could and would take care of her hurt part. She explained to her 10- to 12-year-old exile that she could now lean on the other parts, and especially the Self, for support.

INVITATION

When an exile has been retrieved, given a do-over, and unburdened, there is newly freed space for bringing back some of those qualities of the part that were squashed by the burdens taken on by the exile. This takes the form of an invitation. For my adult client, who was a preteen when she was sexually abused, she had to relinquish playfulness and fun so that she could carry her burden of shame. Part of our healing work means inviting those qualities back into the system.

The IFS model offers a number of activities for inviting a young exile to express the qualities that they didn't get a chance to express or experience when they were younger (Schwartz & Sweezy, 2020). For instance, an exile can verbally integrate positive qualities or can externalize those positive qualities by drawing or creating a sandtray. The client can state a sentiment such as "I would like to invite connection in place of loneliness" to verbally integrate positive qualities. To support the externalization of this, I invite my clients to draw a family to represent connection. The drawing then represents what is inside the system.

INTEGRATION OF CHANGES

In the last of the healing steps for the exile—integration of changes—we strive to understand all the ways the different parts have changed in response to the unburdening. Whenever an exile is unburdened, all parts will change, and sometimes radically. For instance, a firefighter part who worked to protect the exile from the system's scrutiny may find that it no longer needs to deploy a dramatic temper tantrum for protection. But once the exile no longer needs to be hidden away, and attention no longer needs to be diverted from their shame, how will this firefighter act?

For my adult client, integrating changes required us to refocus on the protector parts we worked with in conjunction with the 6 Fs. Consequently, we found and focused on each protector again, inquiring about their feelings and plans for moving forward now that the exile had been unburdened. The goal is not for the protector to go away from the system; instead, we want to allow all protectors to relax and abandon extreme behaviors that contribute to an imbalanced, unintegrated system (Schwartz & Sweezy, 2020). As I've already argued, we need all of our parts—there are no bad parts—but we don't need them to control our system: We have our Self for that.

Conclusion

Ultimately, the flow of IFS is structured by our efforts to truly get to know each client's parts and to support the client as they build relationships among and between their parts and their fundamental Self. Our relationship-building efforts also establish the trust that gives us access to the exiles. Once we understand where the exiles are, we can work to hear their stories and unburden their beliefs. This process will likely have to be repeated several times, and there may be more than one exile that needs unburdening. However, the work of unburdening opens up the space that allows the Self to guide the exile to its neutral nature. When the exile is unburdened and Self-led, the other parts can inhabit their own neutral nature as well.

CHAPTER 4

Play Therapy

Play therapy has a rich and evolving history, rooted in the belief that play is a child's natural language and essential for emotional expression and healing. The foundations of play therapy can be traced to the early 20th century, with significant contributions from pioneers in psychology and child development.

In particular, Anna Freud and Melanie Klein were instrumental in shaping the early approaches to working with children therapeutically. Anna Freud, the daughter of Sigmund Freud, expanded psychoanalytic techniques to address the needs of children, recognizing the importance of understanding their inner worlds through observation and interaction. Melanie Klein, on the other hand, introduced the concept of play as a means for children to express their unconscious thoughts and feelings, laying the groundwork for future therapeutic play models (Landreth, 2024).

Virginia Axline, who was greatly influenced by Carl Rogers, further developed play therapy in the mid-20th century. For many therapists, Rogers is a familiar name because of his association with positive psychology, or person-centered therapy, which he developed during the 1940s. Rogers's approach was marked by his adherence to what he called "unconditional positive regard," which is the conviction, communicated by the therapist to the client, that the therapist accepts the client without judgment, regardless of what the client does or does not express (and whether or not the therapist agrees or disagrees with those expressions).

Axline adapted Rogers's approach, and particularly his concept of unconditional positive regard, into her own model for nondirective play therapy. According to Axline (1947), the therapist must create a safe and welcoming place where the child feels no sense of judgment and feels instead accepted just as they are. She emphasized empathy, acceptance, and the belief that children have the capacity to find solutions to their own problems if given the right environment. Her groundbreaking 1964 book, *Dibs in Search of Self*, remains a cornerstone in the field, illustrating the power of play as a medium for healing.

Over the years, practitioners such as Charles Schaefer, Gary Landreth, and Terry Kottman have contributed significantly to the growth and refinement of play therapy. Schaefer is known for his work in defining and categorizing various play therapy techniques, while Landreth has focused on advancing child-centered approaches and training therapists worldwide. Kottman has been pivotal in the creation of Adlerian play therapy and educating other therapists with the League of Extraordinary Adlerian Play Therapists (LEAPT). The work of these and others led to the development of a broad and versatile model that can be adapted to various populations and integrated with other forms of therapy. Today, play therapy continues to evolve, blending traditional techniques with contemporary insights to better serve children and families across different cultural and social contexts.

While the Association for Play Therapy (APT) offers a definition of play therapy that is grounded in theory and evidence-based practice, I define it more practically, using the words of Kottman & Meany-Walen (2016). Play therapy is:

> an approach to communicating therapeutically with clients using toys, art materials, games, sandtrays, and other play media, giving clients a safe and nurturing relationships in which they can explore and express feelings, gain insight into their own motivation and into their interaction with others, and learn and practice socially appropriate behaviors. (p. 1)

A client-centered definition of play therapy simply describes it as a method that uses a child's natural language of play to decrease the impact of trauma and increase their emotional well-being. As an evidence-based practice, play therapy is thought to be most effective for children under the age of 10 (Senko & Bethan, 2019), which may reflect the language faculties that children gain as they grow. Despite this, 10 years old is not a hard limit: With creativity, play therapy can be used with children of all ages and all developmental stages. In my practice, I've even successfully used it with adults.

It's important to also differentiate between play *in* therapy and *play therapy*. An example of play *in* therapy would be playing a game of UNO™ with a child while also having a talk therapy session with them. However, that same game of UNO can become a therapeutic intervention that constitutes play therapy if, for instance, when playing a "skip" card, the therapist initiates a discussion of a time when the child felt left out or skipped over. In this case, the card is used as a springboard to process the child's thoughts and feelings about the event.

In contrast to the more focused qualities of play therapy, playing *in* therapy casts a wider net. This umbrella term encompasses the use of play and creative activities in therapeutic settings, and it is applicable to individuals of all ages. The spectrum of playing *in* therapy ranges from drawing and painting to music and games, and there is a versatile array of tools therapists can use for exploration.

Nondirective Play Therapy

As you can see, play therapy is systematic and therapeutic, and it can turn a traditional game or activity into an interaction with therapeutic benefits. Importantly, play therapy techniques can be directive or nondirective. Nondirective play therapy, also known as child-centered or person-centered play therapy, makes no effort to control or change the child. It assumes that the child's behavior is driven by the forces of growth and healing (Landreth, 2024). When we use nondirective play therapy techniques, we present with no agenda and allow our client to lead the session.

In this nondirective approach, we take a less active but still an important role (Haas & Ray, 2020). This is what allows the child to lead the play sessions. We focus our efforts on creating a safe and supportive environment for the child to express themselves freely through play. This approach is based on the belief that children, much like adults, have an innate ability to work through their issues and promote healing when allowed to explore and express themselves in a nondirective way.

KEY FEATURES OF NONDIRECTIVE PLAY THERAPY

- **Child-led play:** In nondirective play therapy, the child is encouraged to choose the toys and activities they want to engage with during the sessions. The therapist observes and follows the child's lead, allowing them to express themselves through play in a way that feels natural to them.

- **Unstructured environment:** The play therapy space is deliberately kept unstructured to allow for maximum creativity and self-expression. A variety of toys and materials, such as dolls, action figures, art supplies, and games, may be provided for the child to use freely.

- **Therapist observation:** The therapist observes the child's play behavior, paying attention to themes, patterns, and expressions that may emerge. Through careful observation, the therapist gains insights into the child's emotions, thoughts, and experiences.

- **Reflection and empathy:** The therapist reflects the child's feelings and experiences without judgment. Empathetic responses from the therapist help create a supportive and validating environment, fostering trust and a sense of emotional safety.

- **Expression of feelings:** Nondirective play therapy provides a space for children to express a wide range of emotions, including joy, anger, sadness, and fear. The therapeutic process allows the child to work through and make sense of their emotions in a developmentally appropriate manner.

- **Symbolic play:** Children often use symbolic play to represent their thoughts and feelings. This can involve creating stories, using toys to act out scenarios, or engaging in imaginative play that serves as a metaphor for their experiences.

Ultimately, the therapist's role here is to provide a secure and accepting space, offer unconditional positive regard, and support the child's journey of self-discovery and emotional healing. Nondirective play therapy is particularly suitable for children who find it challenging to express themselves verbally. It allows these children in particular an ability to communicate and process their emotions in a natural and age-appropriate way.

Directive Play Therapy

In contrast to nondirective or child-centered play therapy, where the child leads the play and the therapist observes and interprets, directive play therapy involves the therapist providing structure, guidance, and specific activities to address therapeutic goals. Directive play therapy techniques differ from nondirective ones in that they call on the therapists to take an active, guiding role. Directive play therapy often requires more planning on the part of therapists, particularly in terms of coordinating activities with a particular focus in order to reach a goal, or in terms of actively creating spaces for learning (Kaduson & Schaefer, 2016).

This approach is often used when there's a need for more explicit intervention, when specific issues or behaviors need to be addressed, or when the child may benefit from more guidance and structure in the therapeutic process. It can be especially effective in helping children who may have difficulty expressing themselves or who may benefit from a more focused and goal-directed approach to therapy.

KEY FEATURES OF DIRECTIVE PLAY THERAPY

- **Therapist guidance:** In directive play therapy, the therapist actively directs and guides the play sessions. The therapist may suggest specific activities, themes, or interventions based on the therapeutic goals and the child's needs.

- **Structured activities:** The play sessions involve structured activities designed to address specific issues or challenges the child is facing. These activities may include games, art projects, storytelling, role-playing, or other creative tasks chosen to promote expression and exploration in a targeted way.

- **Goal-oriented approach:** Directive play therapy is goal-oriented, meaning that the therapist and child work together to achieve specific therapeutic objectives. These goals may relate to emotional expression, problem-solving, communication skills, or other areas of concern.

- **Therapeutic techniques:** The therapist may use a variety of therapeutic techniques within the context of play to help the child process emotions, develop coping skills, and gain insights into their thoughts and behaviors. These techniques are often tailored to the individual needs of the child.

- **Active participation:** The therapist actively participates in the play alongside the child, providing support, encouragement, and gentle guidance as needed. This active involvement helps create a therapeutic alliance and enhances the child's sense of safety and trust in the therapeutic relationship.

- **Flexibility:** While directive play therapy provides structure, it also allows for flexibility. Therapists may adjust their approach based on the child's responses, interests, and emerging therapeutic needs.

Both directive and nondirective play therapy techniques can present opportunities for children to express their thoughts and feelings, and for us to assist in moving them from hurt to healing. Both techniques also help to powerfully enhance and repair attachment with both the external and internal systems of the child's world. All play therapy techniques can be implemented in a variety of settings and with a variety of different tools. Different approaches are united by a foundational belief that play is every child's natural method of communication. Through play, play therapists like me maintain that children can express themselves and communicate their feelings and their experiences.

Over the years of my professional career, I have benefited from play therapy–focused training by some of the leaders in play therapy. However, I vividly remember my realization that despite this focus, I was not going to be able to uniformly operate as a child-centered play therapist. I sat in a child-centered play therapy training and listened to the trainer with a growing sense that everything they said *not* to do as a child-centered play therapist was something that I did with the client in my office. For example, the trainer indicated we should *not* refrain from providing directives at all in the play therapy setting and that we shouldn't simply allow our client to play with whatever was available. Similarly, we should always track the child's play, particularly their verbal interactions in play.

As I sat in that training, I felt a cold recognition: I often allowed children to play with whatever was available. I frequently allowed children who wanted to play in complete silence to do so. I felt parts of my protective system come up and whisper, *You are not a good play therapist. You are not following the gospel of play therapy.* At the same time, I knew that my experience and the experience of my clients verified the legitimacy of my work.

Let me take a moment and be clear and transparent here: I love all models of play therapy and have the utmost respect for their creators. However, I have also realized that some of these models and some of the methods associated with these models simply don't fit all the children I see in my office. When I work with certain populations—for example, populations of color—being more directive than allowed by the limited directive techniques of play therapy can sometimes be more beneficial for my client.

This is why I like to say I'm an *integrative play therapist*. While I proceed from an Adlerian play therapy foundation, I integrate a little of this and a little of that from different play therapy training and methods. I had the wonderful opportunity to train in Adlerian play therapy under Dr. Terry Kottman, its creator. At that time, and still today, the Adlerian methods speak most truly to me and to my clinical experience.

Adlerian play therapy is a therapeutic approach that integrates principles from Adlerian psychology into the practice of play therapy. Named after Alfred Adler, the famous Austrian psychiatrist and psychotherapist, Adlerian psychology emphasizes the importance of understanding an individual within their social context and exploring the significance of community, family dynamics, and the pursuit of social interest or contribution to others. Adlerian play therapy adapts these concepts to the context of working with children through play.

KEY FEATURES OF ADLERIAN PLAY THERAPY

- **Holistic perspective:** Adlerian psychology takes a holistic approach, considering individuals within the context of their family and community. In Adlerian play therapy, the therapist considers the child's social context, family dynamics, and community influences when interpreting their play behavior and addressing therapeutic goals.

- **Encouragement and social interest:** Adler emphasized the importance of encouragement and social interest, as well as the idea that individuals naturally strive to contribute positively to their social environment. In Alderian play therapy, the therapist encourages the child's efforts and achievements during play, fostering a sense of competence and social interest.

- **Goal-oriented approach:** Adlerian psychology encourages goal setting and a forward-looking approach to overcoming challenges. In Adlerian play therapy, we set clear therapeutic goals, working with the child to address specific concerns or issues through play.

- **Collaboration and equality:** Adlerian therapy values collaboration and views the therapeutic relationship as a partnership between therapist and client. In Adlerian play therapy, we emphasize collaboration between the child and ourselves, as therapists, promoting an equal and cooperative relationship.

- **Encouragement of responsibility:** Adlerian psychology highlights the importance of fostering a sense of responsibility and accountability. In Adlerian play therapy, we encourage the child to take responsibility for their actions and choices, promoting a sense of empowerment.

- **Exploration of family dynamics:** Adlerian psychology often explores family dynamics and birth order as influential factors in an individual's development. In Adlerian play therapy, we might explore family themes and dynamics through play activities, which can provide insight into the child's experiences within their family system.

- **Use of play as communication:** Adlerian therapy recognizes the importance of communication in understanding individuals. In Adlerian play therapy, as with most other models of play therapy, play is considered a natural form of communication for children. Like all models of play therapy, it emphasizes play activities to facilitate communication and expression.

While Adlerian play therapy is adapted to the developmental needs of children (as with most models of play therapy), it incorporates the various principles of Adlerian psychology. The result is a flexible therapeutic framework that considers the child's unique context, encourages positive social interactions, and works toward the child's psychological well-being and development (Kottman & Meany-Walen, 2016).

The Toys and Tools I Use in Play Therapy

When play is the medium of therapeutic communication, therapists prioritize play in every aspect of their work. In my practice, I tend to encourage play in three ways:

1. By actively focusing on offering children a safe and brave space for play

2. By repeatedly supplying children with different types of toys and mediums for play, such as expressive arts materials and sandtray

3. By strongly supporting children through the process of building a therapeutic relationship with me and with themselves, through which we can interpret their play in a meaningful way

With the help of these elements, children (and even some adults) will almost always engage in various types of play, will almost always express their challenges through their play, and will very often use elements of play to work out different ways of understanding, processing, and overcoming these challenges. Let's take a look at a case vignette drawn from my clients and from the sandtray tool (which I will discuss in the following chapter) to see how this plays out.

Seven-year-old Addy, according to her parents, presented with anxiety and fear due to being physically abused by a babysitter for an extended period of time. While in the playroom, Addy did not talk about her abuse at the hands of her babysitter and, initially, her play did not seem to be related to her traumatic experiences. Though Addy was drawn to the sandtray and often created stories using it, when I attempted to process her stories, investigating whether there were any metaphors in them that might potentially relate to her experiences, I couldn't make any connections.

I chose not to give Addy any sandtray instructions that were more directive than *build what you want*. Instead, I focused on building and strengthening the therapeutic relationship and trusting her ability to meet her own needs through play during our sessions.

After five weeks of storytelling in the sandtray, Addy looked at me at the beginning of one of our sessions and said, "Thanks for listening to my stories." I reassured her that I would always listen to her, regardless of what she decided to share, and she then offered to tell me her story in the sandtray. Over the next several weeks, she took her time to share her experiences with her babysitter with me, and we were then able to discuss her anxiety and fears. Although the sessions started out nondirective in the sandtray, as Addy grew more comfortable through her play, we shifted to more directive sandtray activities, and I gave her prompts to help her build her experiences.

While I find sandtray activities to be particularly useful in my practice, I—and all play therapists—prioritize a variety of play activities by filling our toolbox with several play therapy tools, including the playroom itself, the sandtray, LEGO bricks, art materials, and costume and puppet activities.

The playroom is probably the most important feature of our work because it functions as an invitation to our kids to come and play. The playroom is a safe space, which means children can come in and just be themselves, exploring and communicating in their own way and in different ways over time. We want our clients to enter the playroom and immediately feel not only comfortable but also free and encouraged to be themselves. We want our kids to enter the playroom and *want to play*.

Many play therapists—myself included—find stocking the playroom to be one of the most fun and satisfying aspects of our work. As I already mentioned, sometimes a part (or parts) of me gets caught up in all the toys I want, not just for my clients, but for the child parts of me! Consequently, my playroom is stocked with a range of toys, games, and art supplies, all of which my clients can use in whatever way they choose.

It's not always about packing a playroom, however. A playroom with too many toys and things to do can overwhelm clients or make it too difficult for clients to decide and settle into an activity. For these reasons, play therapists often rotate toys in and out of the playroom. Toys that are new to a client can pique their interest and encourage their play in new ways or offer new ways to play out familiar scenarios. Some therapists might instead use multi-playroom offices, where each room relates to a particular age range.

Generally, the items in the playroom invite certain types of play. Although the items may differ, they usually include the following:

- **Objects to facilitate sandtray therapy:** Sandtray therapy allows a child to create scenes in a miniature sandbox using small figures and objects. In my practice, this allows the child to use their creativity to talk about their experiences. This is just what Addy did during her time with me in the playroom. As it functioned in my work with Addy, the sandtray can be used to build trust and therapeutic relationships, as well as to help to externalize hard experiences.

- **Objects to facilitate expressive art therapy:** With these drawing, painting, coloring, and clay materials, a child can use art to express themself. In my practice, expressive art therapy can take the form of doing quick draws, painting pictures, and sculpturing clay. For instance, a quick draw encourages the child to quickly draw a picture to express themselves, without stopping to perfect their work. With paint, a child can create a scene on paper to express themself or can take advantage of the fluidness of the paint to represent their emotions. Clay can encourage a child to embody the clay and let their hands create.

- **Objects to facilitate puppet play or costume play:** These objects allow children to use puppets to act out scenes and stories. Although puppet play is not one of my preferred activities in my playroom, it has its place. It's not that I don't find it effective, it's because it doesn't always suit my style. That said, puppets can allow children to speak through the puppet or to take on the role of the puppet to tell a story. For some children, it is easier for me to talk directly to the puppet and ask the puppet the harder questions. This can alleviate some of the pressure the child may feel as a result of receiving the therapist's full attention. Costume play, meanwhile, can encourage a child to embody a character or person in order to tell or act out a story.

- **Objects or media to facilitate storytelling:** Storytelling can look many different ways in the playroom. For instance, sometimes storytelling looks like the therapist or child using objects in the playroom to make a child's story come to life. Sometimes, it looks like the therapist telling a story that is similar to the child's experience. Other times, it might even look like nothing therapeutic at all, and instead just function as a fun way to connect with a child and build a therapeutic relationship. Storytelling is also an effective tool for encouraging clients to relax and be creative, regardless of how silly they (or you!) might think you sound. This may be a growing edge for some therapists.

My own playroom, as an extension of my Playful Parts approach, is always stocked with sandtrays, LEGO bricks, child-centered play therapy toys (e.g., dollhouses and figurines, toolsets, dress-up items, cash register and play money, play kitchen set with play foods, stuffed animals, puppets, foam swords and shields, and a variety of other toys), PLAYMOBIL® expressive sets, and a variety of miniatures. I also ensure there are plenty of artsy tools available—from colored pencils, markers, and crayons to oil pastels, paint, and clay—so that my clients can engage in a wide spectrum of creative expressions, including all of the activities I described previously. In this, I follow the research that suggests that different artistic mediums are associated with varying levels of openness and emotional exploration (Hinz, 2020).

As you reflect on how to build out your own therapeutic playroom with expressive art materials, consider consulting the following resources:

- Malchiodi, C. A. (2003). *The art therapy sourcebook*. McGraw Hill. This book explores the various tools and techniques in art therapy and their therapeutic effects.

- Rubin, J. A. (2016). *Approaches to art therapy: Theory and technique* (3rd ed.). Routledge. This resource examines different art therapy approaches, including how mediums influence emotional openness.

- Hinz, L. D. (2020). *Expressive therapies continuum: A framework for using art in therapy* (2nd ed.). Routledge. Hinz provides a detailed explanation of how various art materials align with different emotional states and therapeutic goals.

- Mehlomakulu, C. (2013, January 28). *Media choices in therapy*. https://creativityintherapy.com/2013/01/media-choices-in-therapy. This article discusses the connection between artistic mediums and emotional expression in therapeutic settings.

The Child-Therapist Relationship in Play Therapy

If you ask a group of play therapists what makes for a great play therapy session, you'll get a lot of answers. But successful play therapy—therapy that facilitates communication, enhances social relationships, and increases personal strengths—happens when kids comfortably engage with any of the toys, objects, and games *and with their therapist*.

While the playroom and the techniques and toys definitely contribute to successful play therapy sessions, it's the therapist's support, especially our use of observation and reflection, that ensures our success. Typically, we communicate this support through play therapy toys and tools. Through these, we prioritize creating a safe and brave space for the child to be present, listening to a child's experiences, and showing that we are able hold their stories and continue to make them feel comfortable regardless of how "bad" the experience is (Landreth, 2024).

We do this by attuning ourselves to our client, closely observing their play, and looking for patterns and themes that may emerge. For example, when a client engages in nondirective play, shows aggression, and then moves on to comfort and care, we might observe that the child has witnessed a pattern of abuse that leads to some level of comforting afterward. This can be quite common when, for example, a child has a personal experience of physical abuse but then receives dinner from their abuser (Kestly, 2014).

Metacommunication

Although our observations will certainly enter our conversation with our client, they do not, cannot, and should not interfere with their play. In fact, play therapists typically observe and share their observations using metacommunication, which in Adlerian play therapy refers to the process of talking about the communication itself—essentially, reflecting on or discussing the underlying meaning, patterns, and dynamics of the interactions between the therapist and the child. It's a way to bring awareness to how messages are being sent and received, and it fosters insight and clarity. For example, if a child consistently avoids eye contact or changes the subject during play, the therapist might gently reflect, "I notice when we talk about your feelings, you like to switch to a different game. I wonder what that might mean?" This form of metacommunication helps the child recognize their own patterns, promoting self-awareness and opening space for deeper therapeutic work.

Metacommunication like this aligns with Adlerian core principles of providing encouragement, fostering insight, and developing social interest by helping the child understand how their behaviors and emotions are connected to their experiences and relationships (Kottman & Meany-Walen 2016). The following client example shows metacommunication in action. When working with 9-year-old Maya in the sandtray during her session, I noticed that she frequently buried toy figures in the sand and then immediately dug them up.

> **ME:** I see you've buried that little figure again, just like last time. And now you're digging it right back up.
>
> **MAYA:** Yeah. I just like doing that.
>
> **ME:** Hmm . . . I wonder if the little figure knows it's going to be buried and found again. It seems like it happens a lot.
>
> **MAYA:** Maybe. I guess it likes hiding, but not for too long.
>
> **ME:** It sounds like the figure feels safe hiding but also wants to come back out. Do you ever feel like that—wanting to hide sometimes but also hoping someone finds you?
>
> **MAYA:** Yeah . . . at school sometimes.
>
> **ME:** That makes sense. I wonder if when you bury the figure, it's kind of like giving it a break, but you're always there to help it come back. Just like how you'd want someone to notice you.

MAYA: Yeah. I don't like being forgotten.

ME: That's important to know. We can keep helping the figures together—making sure they know they're not alone, even when they need to hide for a little while

In this example, metacommunication served as a bridge between symbolic play and real-life experiences. By gently reflecting on Maya's actions in the sandtray, I invited her to explore deeper emotions in a non-threatening way. This process helped Maya feel seen and understood, reinforcing encouragement, connection, and insight.

My use of metaphor and curiosity also allowed Maya to project her feelings onto the toys, creating a safe space to process emotions that might otherwise feel too overwhelming to address directly. The interaction not only promoted self-awareness but also strengthened the therapeutic alliance, empowering Maya to gradually express and make sense of her experiences. By engaging in metacommunication, I modeled empathy and helped Maya develop a greater understanding of her own needs and desires.

KEY USES OF METACOMMUNICATION IN PLAY THERAPY

- **Symbolic play:** Children often use symbolic play to represent their thoughts, feelings, and experiences. This can include using toys, objects, or actions as symbols for real-life situations. Therapists use metacommunication to analyze the symbolic elements of play to interpret the underlying meaning and gain insight into the child's internal world.

- **Themes and patterns:** Play therapy sessions may reveal recurring themes or patterns in a child's play behavior over time. Therapists use metacommunication to identify these themes and, through them, understand the concerns, conflicts, or emotions that may be influencing the child's behavior.

- **Role-playing:** Children often engage in role-playing activities during play therapy, taking on different roles or personas. Therapists use metacommunication to observe role-playing and explore the roles chosen by the child, examining how they relate to the child's self-concept, relationships, or experiences.

- **Narrative and storytelling:** Children may use play to create narratives or stories that reflect their thoughts or feelings. Therapists use metacommunication to analyze the content and structure of these narratives to gain insight into the child's cognitive and emotional processing.

- **Use of materials:** The selection and manipulation of play materials (toys, art supplies, etc.) can convey information about the child's preferences, interests, and emotions. Therapists make use of metacommunication by considering the choices made by the child in terms of materials and how they are used and by interpreting their significance in the therapeutic context.

- **Emotional expression:** Play provides a medium for the expression of emotions, including those that may be difficult for the child to verbally articulate. Therapists use metacommunication to observe and interpret the emotional content of play to understand the child's emotional experiences and help them process and regulate emotions.

- **Contextual factors:** The setting, timing, and sequence of play activities contribute to the overall context of metacommunication. Therapists use metacommunication to consider the contextual factors to understand how the child's play relates to their broader experiences and external influences.

Metacommunication is a dynamic process that involves our ongoing observation, interpretation, and reflection. Sometimes, it's only by delving into the symbolic and metaphorical aspects of play that we can uncover meaningful insights, promote therapeutic understanding, and tailor interventions to address the unique needs of the child.

As with other forms of therapy, the relationship between therapist and client is critically important. This is of course true for all clients, but it's particularly true for kids because they rely almost wholly on their therapist for guidance and support through the therapeutic process. When the therapeutic relationship is strong, the child benefits.

Play Therapy and IFS

Play therapy and IFS are two distinct therapeutic approaches that can be used separately, but in my experience, they complement each other when thoughtfully integrated by a trained therapist with knowledge of both models.

In fact, play therapy, whether nondirective or directive, whether Adlerian or not, is a natural partner for IFS. With the two models in use, we can use *play* to communicate and enact the tenets of IFS, particularly its emphasis on our different *parts*. Yes, parts language can sometimes baffle kids—initially, they can be pretty confused when I ask them about their *parts*. But it's this lack of intuitive understanding of concepts like Self and parts that makes the intersection of IFS and play so educational and creative. We already know that play is an essential component of helping children process life experiences. Pairing it with IFS allows children to engage in play to develop internal awareness and healing.

Whereas play therapy is primarily used with kids (although it can be adapted for adolescents and adults), and IFS is typically used with adults (though it can be adapted for adolescents and older children), a therapist skilled in *both* can integrate play therapy techniques into the IFS framework when working with kids. The adaptation recognizes the developmental needs of children and incorporates play as a means of exploring and expressing various internal parts.

Let's take a look at a very general example. Recall that IFS understands that distressing feelings are often held by the vulnerable parts we call exiles. In play therapy, exile parts can be externalized as a doll or an object, and the child can be guided to get to know the exile that carries painful emotions. After further play, the child's protectors may be able to permit us to move more closely to the exile, which can allow the child to witness the exile's past and current experiences by telling their story. This story offers a different, but no less effective, form for the trauma narrative.

Play therapy offers a variety of other useful tools that can help children externalize and symbolize their internal parts, like toys or drawings that kids can use to represent different aspects of themselves or their experiences. But of course, combining play therapy and IFS requires a nuanced understanding of the client's needs.

I gauge these needs during every session. In fact, a Playful Parts session starts like any other therapy session—with a client check-in. Typically, I check in on the thoughts and feelings shared in a previous session, or I ask about my client's experiences over the prior week. I then ask them what they want to focus on in this session, and we start the therapeutic process from there. For me, this process begins with the first Fs: find, focus, and feel.

For example, Samantha, age 15, initially presented with depression. During a session check-in, she told me that she'd had a rough week at school and at home, in part because she'd struggled with intrusive thoughts. She shared that she'd felt really sad and had a hard time feeling happy about anything. I wanted to guide Samantha to *find* the part of her that voiced her intrusive thoughts, so I asked her, "Do you know what part of you was having the intrusive thoughts?"

Samantha responded, "I think it was the depressed part." I then asked her if it would it be okay for us to put some *focus* on that part, and she thought that would be okay. I replied, "When you put your focus on the part, do you *feel* it in your body?" Samantha responded that yes, she did, and that she felt it in her chest. I told her to continue to *focus* on the part. Then, I asked how she *felt* toward the part. Samantha responded, "I care about it."

I suggested to Samantha that she let the part know that she cared about it. Then, I asked her how that part would like to be presented while we get to know it. She stated that she'd like to draw it. Samantha then used the playroom's oil pastels and paper to create the following drawing of the part.

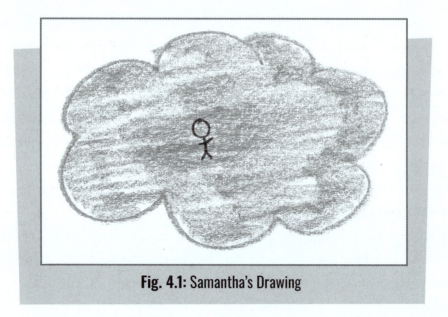

Fig. 4.1: Samantha's Drawing

Once the part was on paper, I again asked Samantha how she felt toward it now, seeing it on paper. She said that was curious about how it looked. I directed her to *focus* on the art as though it were a person connected to her and to then think about how it looked and what it wanted her to know. At this point, Samantha got really quiet for a while, so I waited for her to consider her thoughts. She then started writing in her office journal—the journal she kept at my office—about what the part had shared with her. After getting permission from Samantha, I read it back to her in her own words: "The part is tired of not being happy and wants the sun to shine on it and not have all the darknesses."

Next, I guided Samantha toward *befriending* her part. I asked her to ask the part about this darkness—to just be curious about anything the part wanted her to know. Samantha created another picture. While watching her draw, I noticed that she illustrated a little girl and then covered her with dark clouds. I noted that it looked like the cloud was protecting the little girl by covering her up. Samantha responded that this was the case. I then asked Samantha to continue expressing curiosity about the cloud-protecting behaviors: "Does the cloud like doing its job?" I asked.

"No," reported Samantha.

"What would the cloud rather be doing?"

"It'd rather turn from dark to light," Samantha said.

For the rest of the session, Samantha and I used expressive arts to continue to focus on befriending and building the Self-to-part relationship. This allowed Samantha to express the Self's curiosity to get to know the part and how it protected the exile. Over time, as Samantha continued to work in the playroom on building a relationship with her clouds, I started to see a shift in her artwork and noticed the clouds moving to different locations on the page to eventually show the little girl that represented a very tender part of Samantha's system.

Since Samantha was 15, she was interested in and able to discuss her parts in pretty straightforward ways. This is not always the case, especially when it comes to younger children. A Playful Parts session for young kids can look a lot different. For instance, the check-in is often just as focused on what parents and caregivers have reported to me as it is on the child's feedback. After check-in, the session frequently shifts to nondirective play, during which time I follow and track the child's play.

Let's look to Tyler as an example. Tyler, age 5, presented with anger and destructive behaviors at home and school. Before the session began, Tyler's father reported that Tyler had been sent home three times during the week due to his behaviors. Consequently, when starting the session, I noted to Tyler that it sounded like the school week had been hard. He nodded and shared that he did not listen and got in trouble and had to go home. Using *direct access*, I said to Tyler, "It was hard for you to listen while in school, and your teacher called your dad."

At this point, Tyler began playing with the PLAYMOBIL school, and I began to track his play. Tyler used the models to represent himself and his friends within the school setting and played out interactions between him and his teacher. I continued to speak directly to the part of Tyler that had a hard time listening. Close to the end of the session, I asked this part what we could do to help him listen better in school.

"I don't know," Tyler said.

"What can your teacher do to help you listen better?" I asked.

"Maybe she can move me to the front of the room?" suggested Tyler.

This session looks different from Samantha's session, primarily because of Tyler's age. With Tyler, I spent time using direct access to help Tyler build a Self-to-part relationship so he could get to know the part that had trouble listening. After our session, I spoke with Tyler's father about Tyler's suggestion to move to the front of the class, and his father agreed that he could speak to the teacher. Before our next session, Tyler's father reported that he did not receive any calls home that week. Although Tyler had had a little trouble listening in school, his overall behaviors were better.

These sessions show how Playful Parts can help a child begin to develop the Self-to-part relationship that is so critical to their harmonious system. Play therapy is inherently suited to kids because it aligns with their natural mode of expression. It provides lots of creative outlets for expression, which can complement the more structured and verbal aspects of IFS. Further, play therapy can facilitate the externalization and representation of internal parts. Children (and some adults) may find it easier to work with and understand the concept of internal parts through creative play or visual means. The reliance in play therapy on symbols and metaphors for interpretation also complements the symbolic nature of IFS. This allows individuals to explore and make sense of their internal system in a more metaphorical and symbolic way. Ultimately, when we join the powerful forces of play therapy and IFS, children benefit.

PLAYFUL PARTS KEY FEATURES

- **Facilitates communication:** Playful Parts creates room for clients to speak their natural language of play.

- **Enhances social relationships:** Playful Parts supports *internal relationships* among the parts and between the parts and the Self, as well as *external relationships* with peers, parents, and other adults. A therapeutic relationship with a clinician who names and believes that the child has a benevolent inner Self that can relate in helpful ways to all the child's parts helps create the safety necessary for exploring and experiencing enhanced social relationship skills (Schaefer & Drewes, 2013).

- **Increases personal strengths:** This approach fosters creative problem-solving, resiliency, moral development, accelerated psychological development, self-regulation, and self-esteem (Schaefer & Drewes, 2013). The combination of play and parts work helps clients develop resiliency by differentiating from their parts that carry challenging feelings and behaviors.

Conclusion

By integrating play therapy and IFS, therapists honor the innate multiplicity of the child's inner world, providing a safe space for parts to emerge and express themselves through play. By blending the non-pathologizing stance of IFS with the creative and expressive nature of play therapy, practitioners can facilitate deep healing and empower children to access their Self-energy—marked by compassion, curiosity, and confidence. The integration not only enriches the therapeutic process but also reinforces the child's resilience and capacity for growth. As therapists work to weave these models together, they cultivate a pathway for lasting transformation, fostering healing that ripples across the child's relationships and life experiences.

CHAPTER 5

Playful Parts Activities: Sandtray

As a play therapist, I see sandtray therapy as a profoundly transformative tool that speaks to the heart of what makes play therapy so powerful—it offers our clients ways to express the inexpressible. In the sandtray, clients of all ages can tell their stories, process emotions, and explore their inner worlds without relying on words. The tactile nature of the sand, combined with the symbolism of miniature figures, creates a space where healing and growth unfold naturally. It is a gentle yet impactful approach that honors the unique experiences of each individual, providing them a safe, nonjudgmental environment in which to navigate their journey toward healing.

Homeyer and Sweeney (2022) define sandtray therapy as an expressive and projective mode of psychotherapy involving the unfolding and processing of intra and interpersonal issues through the use of specific sandtray materials as a nonverbal medium of communication. It must be led by the client or therapist and facilitated by a trained therapist. This method is rooted in the early 20th century, where it drew from psychology, psychoanalysis, and play therapy. The foundational concepts can be traced back to the work of Margaret Lowenfeld, a British child psychiatrist, who in the 1920s developed what she called the "World Technique," a method that allowed children to express their inner experiences by creating worlds in trays of sand using miniature figures. Her work was inspired by her belief that children often communicate best through play and symbolic expression rather than words (Homeyer, 2019).

H. G. Wells may be better known for his contributions to science fiction literature, but he also played a significant role in the early development of therapeutic play through his creation of the "floor games" technique. In 1911, Wells published *Floor Games*, a book describing how he used miniature figures, blocks, and other small objects to create imaginative worlds on the floor with his two sons. Wells believed that this form of play fostered creativity and also allowed children to express their thoughts, emotions, and experiences in a natural and engaging way. His work highlighted the importance of free, unstructured play as a means for children to communicate and explore their inner worlds. Although not developed with formal therapeutic intent, Wells' floor games laid the groundwork for future play therapy techniques, including Margaret Lowenfeld's World Technique and the evolution of sandtray therapy (Wells, 1911).

Lowenfeld opened the Clinic for Nervous and Difficult Children in October of 1928, where she offered trays of sand and a collection of small toys for children to share their inner worlds. In 1937, she presented the World Technique at a clinical conference in Paris (Lowenfeld, 1979). Her method of sand work in therapy continued to grow with the help of Dora Kalff, who studied under Lowenfeld in London in 1956 (Homeyer & Sweeney, 2022).

Kalff integrated Carl Jung's theories of the collective unconscious, symbols, and archetypes into her approach. She believed that the sandtray provided a sacred, nonverbal space where clients could externalize and process unconscious material, facilitating healing and personal growth. Kalff's work emphasized the importance of allowing clients to work freely and without interpretation during sessions, trusting that the psyche's natural tendency toward healing would guide the process. This method became especially influential in child therapy but has since been widely applied to individuals of all ages dealing with trauma, grief, and psychological distress. Kalff's contributions laid the foundation for sandplay therapy as a recognized therapeutic modality, and her teachings continue to influence therapists worldwide (Kalff, 1980).

Sandplay therapy is often seen as rigid because it closely adheres to the principles of Dora Kalff's original Jungian framework, which emphasizes a nondirective, structured process. The rigidity stems from specific guidelines that shape the therapeutic experience, such as the use of a defined tray size, particular types of sand (wet and dry), and a curated collection of miniature figures representing diverse aspects of life and the psyche. The therapist's role is deliberately minimal during the session, serving as an observer rather than an active guide. In theory, the strict structure ensures the client's unconscious can express itself freely without interference or interpretation, aligning with Jungian beliefs about the psyche's capacity for self-healing.

There are broader benefits to this rigidity: It creates a predictable and secure environment that fosters deep psychological work. By limiting external influence, the structured nature of sandplay therapy allows the unconscious to emerge of its own accord, facilitating the integration of unconscious material and promoting individuation—the process of becoming one's true self. This containment can provide a sense of safety, allowing clients to access and resolve inner conflicts or traumas at their own pace, ultimately fostering greater emotional resilience and self-awareness.

However, as play therapy developed and evolved, the use of sand evolved as well. Sandtray has become a more flexible approach. With sandtray, a therapist isn't tied to the more rigid, more limited sandplay model. In fact, because of sandtray's versatility, it can be integrated with various therapy models, including eye movement desensitization reprocessing (EMDR), cognitive behavioral therapy (CBT), Adlerian play therapy, Gestalt therapy, and other theoretical modalities—including, of course, IFS. Using sandtray with various modalities gives the therapist countless methods and techniques to enhance the opportunity for healing with the client. This adaptability allows therapists to actively engage with clients, offering prompts, directives, or reflections as appropriate, fostering a more interactive and dynamic therapeutic process.

The primary benefit of combining sandtray with IFS includes the ability of sandtray therapy to engage the brain on multiple levels, facilitating integration between the emotional, sensory, and cognitive systems. As clients manipulate the sand and arrange miniatures, they activate the right hemisphere, which governs creativity, emotion, and nonverbal processing. This allows for the expression of deep-seated feelings and memories that may be difficult to articulate. At the same time, the left hemisphere, responsible for logic and language, can begin to make sense of the symbolic representations in the tray. This bilateral stimulation helps foster neural integration, promoting healing, emotion regulation, and the processing of trauma. By engaging the whole brain, sandtray therapy supports deeper psychological growth and resilience (Cozolino, 2017).

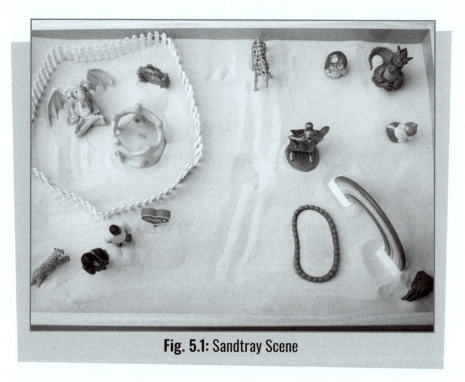

Fig. 5.1: Sandtray Scene

Getting Started with Sandtray

Preparation for using the sandtray requires sand, miniatures, and a tray. The use of sand is purposeful because it serves as a powerful medium for expression and exploration. The tactile, fluid nature of sand allows clients to engage with it in immersive ways that can be both grounding and symbolic. As clients sift, shape, or manipulate the sand, they externalize inner experiences and emotions that may be difficult to express verbally. The sand becomes a canvas where stories, conflicts, and unconscious material can emerge and take form through miniature figures and objects. This process encourages creativity and play and also facilitates deeper self-awareness and insight. The purposeful use of sand enables clients to connect with their inner world in a non-threatening, indirect manner, making it an essential and transformative element in the therapeutic process.

In their sandtray manual, Homeyer and Sweeney (2022) explain that sand is highly symbolic, with an elemental connection to the Earth and to Christianity. The authors cite the Old Testament, Genesis 2:7: "God formed man from the dust of the ground and breathed into his nostrils the breath of life, and man became a living soul." Building on this citation, Homeyer and Sweeney agree that "Our connection to this Earth is foundational. This is not accidental, but rather providential design. As we connect with the sand, we cannot help but feel the connection to the spirit within, and the Creation without" (p. 23).

Of course, the sand is also a practical element and, as such, it shapes the client's experience. Therapists can choose among a wide variety of sands, and many choose more than one, including sands in an assortment of colors and textures. For a different sensory experience, therapists may use uncooked rice and beans too.

After the choice of sand, miniatures must also be supplied. These are the crucial "toys" of the sandtray technique and are especially important for those of us who primarily work with kids. Here, Gary Landreth (2024) bears repeating: "Toys are used like words by children, and play is their language" (p. 12). Miniatures are alternatively called *figures*, *symbols*, and *metaphors* in sandtray therapy. But whatever they're called, they allow clients to express themselves in the sand. Some sandtray experts recommend that therapists have around 300 miniatures for their clients to choose from. However, I've found that fewer miniatures, often just 15 to 20, can ensure that clients aren't overwhelmed by their choices.

Regardless of number, miniatures should be drawn from the following categories:

- **People:** Family groups of various ages and cultures, as well as figures representing brides, grooms, officiants, religious figures, occupational figures, sports figures, historical figures

- **Animals:** Sea life, insects, birds, prehistoric animals, zoo and wild animals, farm and domestic animals

- **Buildings:** Houses, single-family homes, apartment buildings, businesses, churches, temples, mosques, castles, forts, teepees, World Trade Center, military tents, barns

- **Transportation:** Old and new cars, trucks, military vehicles, dump trucks, bulldozers, buses, helicopters, airplanes, spaceships, fishing boats, canoes, yachts, rafts, ocean liners, military landing craft, submarines, rowboats

- **Vegetation:** Trees with and without leaves, autumn trees, palm trees, pine trees, Christmas trees, plants, bushes, cacti, flowers, hedges

- **Fences, gates, signs:** Gates, barricades, street signs, railroad tracks, caution signs

- **Natural items:** Seashells, rocks, sticks, dried flowers, branches, twigs

- **Fantasy:** Magical figures, wizards, witches, wishing wells, dragons, unicorns, gargoyles, sphinx, monsters, cartoon and comic book figures, movie characters, ghosts, phantoms, gnomes

- **Spiritual and mystical:** Figures representing Western and Eastern religious groups and other religions, Buddha, Day of the Dead skeletons, magic or crystal balls, crystals, gold, mirrors, pyramids, and goddesses

- **Landscaping:** Ponds, rainbows, fire, clouds, stars, sun, moon globe, water waves

- **Household items:** Bathtub, furniture, toilet, bed food, kitchen items

- **Miscellaneous items:** Medical items, wine bottles, beer bottles

In addition to items from the preceding list, I like to add what I consider *statement items*, like painted rocks and expression pieces.

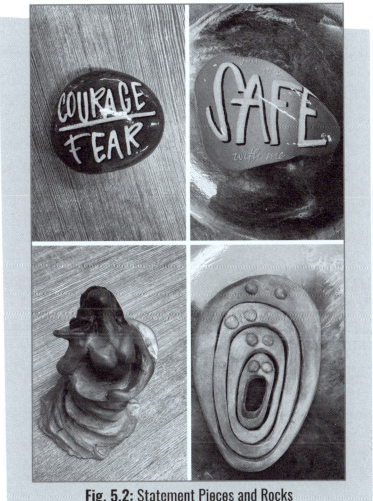

Fig. 5.2: Statement Pieces and Rocks

The tray is perhaps less critical to the client's experience, and there is a lot of flexibility in terms of size and shape. A standard sandtray is 30 inches by 20 inches and 3 inches deep. A standard tray is also painted blue on the bottom to simulate water and blue on the sides to simulate the sky. Sandplay practitioners also recommend having two standard sandtrays available, one dry and one wet, since the textural difference can be a therapeutic aid. Dry sand is light, flowing, and easy to manipulate, and can often represent openness, flexibility, and surface-level exploration. It allows clients to create, shift, and reshape their worlds with ease, mirroring the fluid nature of conscious thoughts and emotions. Wet sand, in contrast, is more solid, moldable, and heavy, and can provide a grounding experience that can facilitate deeper emotional work. Clients may find it easier to build structures, form boundaries, or express containment and stability with wet sand, or they may be able to externalize subconscious material or repressed feelings that are ready to surface. Offering both types of sand gives clients more to work with and more to work with more freely. It also typically makes for a richer, more dynamic environment where clients can engage with their experiences on multiple levels (Homeyer & Sweeney, 2022).

Sandtray in Playful Parts

Sandtray techniques can be used effectively in many ways and in many clinical settings. In Playful Parts, however, the techniques are used to support the Self-to-part relationship with the protective system by using the 6 Fs and working with the exile through the healing steps. Sandtray is particularly helpful in this capacity because sandtray activities can allow clients to gain access to and awareness of their inner world while offering an externalizing intervention. We already know that externalization allows clients to express their parts' inner perceptions and senses, as well as to manifest the internal narratives that belong to these parts. When clients use sandtray activities, they can start to comprehend the ways their parts interconnect and function, potentially even gaining access to their aspirations for these parts and for their interconnections. Externalization makes integration possible.

Despite its promise, and despite the reality that many therapists already successfully use sandtray alongside IFS, there is limited research to guide its implementation. As the popularity of IFS grows, research will follow. For the time being, I've used my training to develop a clinically successful method for deploying sandtray activities to support IFS. The flow is based primarily on the client's internal system, as well as on the 6 Fs and the healing steps. This means that the flow is unique to each client and may or may not reflect more traditional IFS processes. Above all, these healing steps are fluid, iterative rather than linear, and allow for flexibility based on the client's readiness and the dynamics of their internal system.

Before using sandtray as part of Playful Parts, you must have skills in IFS and sandtray methods. However, and as with every element of IFS therapy, you must also have a critical mass of Self to be effective, including:

- Curiosity, and the ability to be open about the client's inner system and how their parts are externalized, as well as an interest in helping the client be open and welcoming to the process of developing the Self-to-part relationship.

- Connectedness, and the ability to therapeutically connect with the client and co-create a space of healing both externally and internally.

- Presence, and the ability to create more room for the client and their process by asking your own parts to give space.

- Patience, and the ability to slow down and be comfortable with silence while the client takes their time to build their trays and process them.

- Playfulness, and the ability to be silly and joyful with parts when applicable.

To prepare to use sandtray, it's important to take time and care to prepare the space and to check in with your parts and invite in your Self-energy. Preparing the space is a critical step that will depend on your client's needs. It includes dictating the number and type of trays and organizing the miniatures. Some clients, particularly those who may already be overwhelmed, may be more comfortable engaging with a smaller selection of trays and a particular set of miniatures, or they may prefer a particular category of miniatures. Others may prefer a wider variety of options. Making these decisions depends on your understanding of your client, as well as on some trial and error.

To check for Self-energy, take a few moments prior to your client arriving for the session to check in with your system to see what parts are present and to ask those parts to give you space to be more present in the room with the client. Think of the 8 Cs—calm, clarity, compassion, curiosity, confidence, courage, creativity, and connectedness—and invite in the 5 Ps of your Self-energy: presence, patience, persistence, playfulness, and perspective. The goal is to go into the session with no agenda so as to be fully present to follow the client's system.

Once the room is prepared and you've checked in with your Self-energy, you're ready to invite your client to the work. At the beginning of the first session, take a few moments to settle the client and orient them to the sandtray space. This can be effectively done with a breathing exercise or meditation. Then, invite them to engage with the sandtray by explaining the purpose and nature of sandtray therapy, highlighting how it allows for the expression of thoughts and emotions that may be difficult to say with words. It's important to normalize the experience, emphasizing that there is no right or wrong way to engage with the sand or miniatures. It's also important to remember that you can introduce the sandtray gradually, inviting the client to explore the sand with their hands first to build familiarity and comfort. By attuning to the client's responses and thoughtfully pacing the introduction to the activity, you foster a sense of safety, increasing the likelihood of a meaningful and transformative sandtray experience. Finally, make sure to explicitly give your client permission to express themself with whatever is in the room and however they want to. This simple offering can have outsize effects and can be especially helpful for kids who don't have a lot of control in their external environments.

Once the client feels grounded and ready, guide them to begin building their sandtray. This process can start with a gentle, open-ended prompt such as "Show me your inner world" or "Create what feels present for you today." Such invitations can encourage clients to intuitively express their thoughts and emotions without overthinking or filtering their responses. For clients who may need more structure or focus, a more directive approach can be used. This might include prompts like "Create a tray that reflects how you are feeling right now" or "Build a scene that represents something you are struggling with." Alternatively, the therapist can tailor a prompt based on the client's current therapeutic goals or what has emerged in previous sessions, allowing the work to unfold in alignment with their process.

You can encourage your client to take their time selecting miniatures and arranging them in the sand, offering reassurance that there is no right or wrong way to proceed. If the client seems hesitant or unsure, reflect on what you observe, gently prompting them with "Let's take a look inside and build a tray based on what you notice." This encourages self-awareness and invites curiosity about internal experiences. For clients focusing on specific outcomes, a directive such as "Create a tray that represents what you hope to express or work through today" can guide the session toward intentional exploration.

Your willingness to shift flexibly between directive and nondirective approaches means you can meet the client where they are. A more directive approach can gently guide clients who may be hesitant or unsure, while a less directive style can encourage deeper exploration and connection to Self-energy.

As your client builds their sandtray, you can thoughtfully reflect aloud on what you observe, with an eye toward creating opportunities for deeper exploration and insight. However, some clients may prefer silence while building their tray, and this is entirely acceptable. The decision is a choice point in the therapeutic process—while one session might benefit from active reflection and dialogue, another might require silent observation to allow the client's internal world to unfold without interruption. Reflections, when appropriate, can extend beyond the tray to include the client's emotional state, body language, or overall engagement. Your words don't need to be exclusively positive, but they should always be compassionate and nonjudgmental, inviting curiosity rather than direction. By staying attuned to the client's needs and pacing the session accordingly, you create an environment that honors your client's process, whether through words or quiet presence.

In sessions that prioritize reflection, your words will slightly mirror child-centered play therapy by tracking the client's building process. For example, when your client is picking miniatures, you might say:

- I'm noticing you are taking your time to pick out miniatures that represent your parts.

- I noticed you continue to look at the tree miniature.

Or when your client is building their tray:

- You're working hard to build the world you want.

- I see you're taking your time to place each miniature in the right place for you.

Once your client has completed building their tray, you will then ask questions that help to operationalize the 6 Fs. For instance, you'll invite them to notice their tray as you give attention to each miniature. You'll then invite them to share what they have in their tray by directing their attention to a particular miniature, or you can invite them to share the narrative or story behind a particular miniature or a miniature of their choosing.

In the next section, I walk you through a sample therapist-client dialogue that illustrates what this can look like. The client in the following dialogue was an 8-year-old boy who struggled with peers in the school setting. Although he came home each day visibly upset, he refused to discuss his challenges with his parents. Instead, he became withdrawn and began to engage in isolating behaviors, such as avoiding conversation and eye contact and retreating to his bedroom, where he'd frequently close and lock the door. The goals with sandtray included supporting the client in identifying the parts that were activated by his school experiences.

FIND

Once my client finished building his sandtray, I invited him to *find* different aspects of the sandtray—including miniatures or objects and configurations and scenes—on which to focus. I began by simply encouraging him to look at his sandtray, to observe what he'd put in it, and as we moved closer to the work of focusing on a target miniature, to start to notice what was happening in his thoughts and his body.

> **Me:** Now that you've finished creating, take a few moments to give attention to each item in your tray.
>
> **Client:** [*nods and looks around the tray*]
>
> **Me:** [*looks at each item in the tray while staying attuned to the client*] Can you tell me about your tray?
>
> **Client:** There is a school, a playground, and kids outside.
>
> **Me:** Ah, I see. Is there anything else you want me to know about what's in your tray?
>
> **Client:** Yes. This is what happens every day at school.
>
> **Me:** Thank you for sharing.

FOCUS

As my client explained the contents of his sandtray, I moved to invite him to find one particular piece in the sandtray on which he would like to *focus*. As therapists, we can proceed directly here, asking clients which piece in the sandtray they want to put their focus on, or we can ask them something like "Which item in the sandtray seems to give off the most energy?" To help clients identify what "energy" might mean in this context, we can ask them to focus on their body and on the sensations they feel when they focus on the different items in the sandtray.

> **Me:** Would it be okay to explore what you've created about being at school every day?
>
> **Client:** Okay.
>
> **Me:** I invite you to look at your tray and let me know what you want to focus more on.
>
> **Client:** [*looks around the tray*] I want to focus on the blue person.

Once the client identifies a miniature on which to focus, we invite them to pick up the miniature and hold it, or to simply put their focus on it by looking at it. Next, we ask questions designed to make the miniature and its role knowable—to the client primarily, but to us too. Of course, clients don't always know—or know *how*—their sandtray items relate to their experiences. We, as therapists, may know that the miniatures to which clients are initially drawn act as protectors, keeping exiles hidden and protected. But our clients don't know this. When we support clients in finding and focusing on a particular miniature, we support their effort to begin to connect with that miniature as a protector, and we encourage the connection by asking questions like "What are you noticing when you put your attention on the miniature?"

> **ME:** I invite you to put all your focus on the blue person. You can hold it if you need to.
>
> **CLIENT:** [*picks up the blue person*]
>
> **ME:** While you are holding it, what are you noticing about it?
>
> **CLIENT:** I'm noticing how it feels in my hand. I also notice a funny feeling in my tummy.
>
> **ME:** Does it seem like the feeling in your tummy is separate from the blue person?
>
> **CLIENT:** It seems like it's the same. Like the blue person and I are sharing a feeling in our tummy.
>
> **ME:** Continue to hold it and put some focus on your tummy.
>
> **CLIENT:** Okay.
>
> **ME:** How is your tummy reacting to you noticing it?
>
> **CLIENT:** [*rubbing blue person's tummy*] When I think about the feeling in my tummy, it goes away.
>
> **ME:** Continue to focus on the blue person.
>
> **CLIENT:** Okay.

FEEL

Moving from finding and focusing to *feeling*, we now ask our client how they *feel toward* the miniature. This is not quite the same as asking about the feelings our client experiences when they simply focus on the miniature. Instead, we're asking our client how they feel *about* the miniature. If our client's Self-energy is present, it will manifest in the expression of one of the 8 Cs, or in a positive statement of some kind. When our client's Self-energy is present, we ask them to extend to their miniature the positive statement they've shared. For instance, if our client responds to our question about how they feel about the blue miniature with a version of "I wonder why he (or she) is standing like that," we can interpret this as an expression of curiosity, one of the 8 Cs of Self-energy. We can then ask our client to expand on this curiosity and extend it to the miniature. This may be a new concept for clients, and we might have to provide some guidance. We can say something as simple as "Send those I'm-interested-in-you vibes to that miniature," or we can take the statement used and ask the client to "share your energy of curiosity with the miniature."

Often, however, there is no Self-energy present, and our client doesn't respond with an expression of one of the 8 Cs or with any kind of positive statement. In this case, something is blocking the client's direct connection to the miniature. We want to help our client consider this by asking them to notice what is blocking that connection. Then, we want to support our client in asking this blocking part to give space so that they can continue to focus on the target miniature and learn more about their feelings about the miniature. Once the client is able to indicate that the miniature has made space, we can ask our client again how they feel toward the miniature.

> **ME:** How are you feeling toward the blue person?
>
> **CLIENT:** What do you mean how I feel toward it?
>
> **ME:** I mean, what are you noticing when you put your attention on it?
>
> **CLIENT:** Oh, you mean what feelings do I have?
>
> **ME:** Yes, exactly.

CLIENT: Well, I don't like him, he's weak.

ME: Can you look past the don't-like and the weakness?

CLIENT: I can try.

ME: Take your time, and look past it because I want to ask you again how you feel toward the blue person.

CLIENT: I feel a little sadness for him, and I care about him.

ME: It's okay to feel that sadness. Can you share the care you have for the blue person with him?

CLIENT: How do I share the care?

ME: You can just let the blue person know that you care about him.

CLIENT: [*smiles*] I let him know that I care.

ME: How did the blue person respond to your care?

CLIENT: He smiled.

ME: [*whispers*] I noticed your smile too.

BEFRIEND

Once the client is able to express a part of their Self-energy toward the target miniature, we can move to *befriending*. Our goal here is to help the client establish a deeper and more meaningful relationship connection between their Self-energy and the miniature that represents the part. The sandtray context makes this work look a little different from traditional IFS because we're using miniatures to present the parts, and our focus is not on directly leaning inward toward the internal system but on indirectly leaning toward the miniature. Nonetheless, we can ask traditional befriending questions like "Does the miniature know that you're here?" or "What's it starting to notice about you?" Your client may not connect to these questions initially. In this case, it can be helpful to invite your client to express curiosity about the miniature through questions like "Does the miniature know who you are? or "Does it know how old you are?" Then, you can invite your client to update the miniature with information.

It's important to remember that befriending is about establishing and deepening trust. To this end, you can ask your client more directive questions like "Does the miniature trust you?" or "What does the miniature need right now from you?" Once your client supplies answers, you can follow up with "How might you let it know you're here to understand it and not judge it?" This allows for gentle connection and starts to build trust between the Self and the part. The effectiveness of these questions, like all others, will of course depend on the age and cognitive processing ability of your client.

ME: Hmm, I'm curious if the blue person knows who you are. Can you check?

CLIENT: Yep, he knows me.

ME: Since he knows who you are, it sounds like you two are connected.

CLIENT: Yeah.

ME: Can you be curious and see how old the blue person thinks you are?

CLIENT: I can—he thinks I'm 5.

ME: Oh, can you let him know that you're 8?

CLIENT: I let him know.

ME: How did he respond to that?

CLIENT: He was like, wow you are old [*laughs*].

ME: [*laughs*] How are you feeling toward the blue person right now?

CLIENT: A lot of love for him.

ME: Is there a miniature that you want to add to your tray to represent that love?

CLIENT: Can I draw a heart in the sand?

ME: Of course, you can! Notice how the blue person responds to the heart.

CLIENT: He likes the heart.

You've by now noticed that sandtray work, as guided by the 6 Fs, is also iterative work. You will frequently ask your client questions that begin with "How do you feel toward . . ." because these questions allow you to check for emerging Self-energy or to check on whether another part is blocking the target part. You may find that you repeat other questions too. One of my IFS colleagues frequently asks, "How openhearted are you to the part?" You, too, can get creative with how you ask these questions, using the language or words of your client. In fact, using a child's words can let their parts know that you, as the therapist, listen to them and pay attention to how they speak and the words they may have used in session.

FIND OUT

Once your client has found and focused on their target miniature in their sandtray scene, identified their feelings about and around this miniature, and begun to establish a deeper and more meaningful connection, it's time to *find out*. Finding out is the means by which we help clients get to know the miniature better and deepen their connection to it. As previously discussed, exploring more about the part aligns with the core IFS belief that all parts hold positive intentions. This is essential to keep in mind and can be gently reinforced with the client as they begin to uncover how and why the part is occupying its place in the system. The stronger the trust and connection between the client and the miniature, the more the part represented by the miniature will reveal about its role.

Here, too, we express a sense of openness and curiosity through find-out questions that, for instance, invite the client to place additional miniatures in the sandtray to express what the target miniature wishes to communicate. Revisiting the sandtray build can also ensure the target miniature continues to feel seen and heard.

Because many of the objects in the sandtray take on a protector role, the following questions are designed to explore the target miniature's fulfillment of this role, including the level of protection it offers and any fears or concerns it may have regarding the exile. You will recognize some of these from chapter 3. As trust and connection grow, the protector can begin to relax, which in turn allows it to share more about the exile's experience.

Although I offer the following list for the purpose of fostering trust and connection, I have to admit that a part of me hesitates because I don't want to restrict readers to a set of formulated questions. It's essential for us, as therapists, to adapt our questions to align with each client's unique system, communication style, and developmental stage. Every client's internal landscape is different, and the way parts express themselves can vary greatly depending on the client's age, emotional maturity, and language abilities. That said, sample questions include:

- What does this miniature want you to know?
- What is this miniature's intention?
- How long has this miniature been doing its job?
- Does it like its job?
- How does it protect you?
- What would it rather be doing?
- What does it need from you?
- How old does it think you are?

For younger clients or those with less verbal processing capacity, questions may need to be simplified, made more concrete, or framed in playful, imaginative terms. For adults, the language might reflect deeper nuance and abstract thought. By tuning into the client's responses and pacing, the therapist ensures that the questions feel accessible and non-threatening, fostering a sense of safety and trust within the system. This flexibility allows the therapist to honor and engage the client's parts in a way that feels natural and appropriate, supporting healing at a level the client can fully embrace.

> **ME:** Would it be okay to get to know the blue person even more?
>
> **CLIENT:** Yes, it's fine.
>
> **ME:** Hmm, I wonder if the blue person has a name? Can you check?
>
> **CLIENT:** It's Max.
>
> **ME:** What does Max want us to know about him at the school and the kids?

CLIENT: He stays away from the kids on the playground at school.

ME: Can you say more?

CLIENT: Staying away from other kids keeps him safe.

ME: How long has he been staying away?

CLIENT: For a while.

ME: I wonder how old Max is.

CLIENT: He's 8 just like me.

ME I wonder how old Max was when he first started staying away.

CLIENT: Since he was 5.

ME: It sounds like Max has been working hard for a while to stay safe.

CLIENT: Yep.

ME: I wonder if he likes staying away.

CLIENT: Nope.

ME: Hmm, I wonder what he rather be doing other than staying away?

CLIENT: He would like to play with the other kids.

FEARS

We want to move toward helping the client find out more about their part's *fears* and concerns, particularly around what would happen if a part didn't do its job. Remember that we fulfill this role as a Hope Merchant, holding hope and belief in the client's healing process, even if the client feels stuck or hopeless. By consistently supporting our client in listening and responding to their part's fears, we get closer to the exiles. The following questions about the target miniature can help provide this kind of support:

- If we could help the miniature feel braver (or less worried), would that sound good to you?

- What if I could promise the miniature it won't get too big or too loud? Would you let me help it a little?

- I know it might seem hard to believe, but if we could make that miniature feel less lonely or scared, would you want to give it a try?
- What if we could help that miniature remember it's not alone anymore? Would that feel better?

Only when all of a client's parts' fears and concerns have been addressed can we turn to working with exiles.

ME: I wonder what Max is afraid would happen if he didn't stay away?

CLIENT: He's scared it will happen again.

ME: Max is working hard to keep himself safe.

CLIENT: Yes he is . . . he doesn't want the other kids to pick on him again.

ME: It makes sense that Max would stay away so that would not happen again.

CLIENT: [*nods head*]

ME: I wonder if Max remembers the first time he started to stay away?

CLIENT: When he was 5 years old one day at recess when he was in kindergarten.

ME: What if I told you we could help 5-year-old Max not be so afraid when on the playground. Would you want to help him?

CLIENT: Yes, I would.

When working with clients, especially children, the therapeutic process may not always reach the deeper steps of engaging with exiles or vulnerable parts. Strong protectors often stand guard, unwilling to grant access to more delicate parts of the system due to fears of overwhelm, re-traumatization, or instability. In some cases, the client may still be actively experiencing trauma, making the protector's role even more rigid and necessary for survival. Additionally, a lack of trust between the client and therapist can prevent meaningful exploration, as the protector may perceive the therapist as a potential threat or someone who could expose the client to painful emotions.

Strong protectors may resist stepping back, even when approached with compassion and curiosity. These parts often carry the belief that they are the only thing holding the system together. Attempts to bypass or push through their defenses can lead to increased resistance or shutdown. Instead, the therapist can focus on building a relationship with the protector, acknowledging its fears, and respecting its role without rushing the process.

In these situations, therapy may center on continuing to develop trust and creating safety, rather than directly accessing the exile. The therapist can gently inquire about the protector's needs and offer appreciation for its hard work, reinforcing the idea that the goal is not to remove the protector but to support it in finding relief. Over time, as the protector feels seen, validated, and less fearful, it may naturally soften and become more open to collaboration. This patient, attuned approach is critical to fostering deeper healing while honoring the pace of the client's system.

If, however, your client is willing, sandtray activities can be a helpful adjunct to the healing steps. Through the creative and symbolic nature of the sandtray, clients can access and strengthen their Self-energy, fostering the compassion and curiosity needed for healing their most vulnerable parts. The sandtray allows clients to witness the exile's pain in a tangible form, facilitating the retrieval of wounded parts. As the exile feels seen and supported, the Self of the client can guide it through the unburdening process, helping it release heavy emotions or beliefs. Finally, the sandtray supports the integration and harmonization of parts, reinforcing new roles and fostering ongoing internal dialogue and balance. This hands-on, visual approach provides a unique pathway to engage with and embody the healing journey, remembering these steps are fluid rather than linear. The next section walks you through each of these healing steps.

The Healing Steps with Sandtray

WITNESSING

Witnessing the exile in the sandtray is a deeply transformative step in the healing process, allowing clients to externalize and engage with their most vulnerable parts in a safe and tangible way. In other play therapy approaches, this is considered the trauma narrative, a psychological technique that helps children make sense of their experiences with trauma through storytelling. By selecting miniatures or objects that represent the exile, clients can give form to the emotions, memories, and burdens that have long been hidden or suppressed. As they arrange the sandtray, we gently guide them to observe the exile with compassion and curiosity, encouraging them to notice how the part feels, what it needs, and the story it carries. This process creates a sense of distance, making the experience feel less overwhelming while fostering deeper empathy and connection. The sandtray provides a visual and symbolic space for the exile to express itself, allowing the client to witness and honor its pain without judgment. Through this witnessing, the exile begins to feel seen, validated, and understood—essential steps toward healing and unburdening.

> **Me:** Eight-year-old Max shared that he wanted to help 5-year-old Max. Can we do that?
>
> **Client:** Yes, we can.
>
> **Me:** I invite you to find a miniature that represents 5-year-old Max.
>
> **Client:** I want to use this red person, and I want to call him Little Max.
>
> **Me:** Would it be okay to learn about what happened to Little Max?
>
> **Client:** I don't know . . . he is a little scared.
>
> **Me:** Would it be okay if you told me what he is scared of?
>
> **Client:** That the kids at school will pick on him again.
>
> **Me:** Ohh, that makes sense. Can you let Little Max know that we just want to hear about what happened at school?
>
> **Client:** He is okay with that.
>
> **Me:** I invite you to use the sandtray to tell Little Max's story.
>
> **Client:** [*builds a sandtray*]
>
> **Me:** Tell me about your tray.

CLIENT: The dragon is a boy who was on the playground and in class.

ME: Would it be okay to tell me more?

Fig. 5.3: Max's Sandtray Scene

CLIENT: When Little Max went to the new school, he was really scared because he didn't know anyone. His teacher was really nice and helped him. When it was time for recess, he wanted to play with the other kids, and one of the boys told him no and called him stupid. When he was back in class, the same boy called him stupid again when he messed up after the teacher asked what colors were on the board.

ME: Is there anything else that Little Max wants us to know?

CLIENT: No.

Once the exile has shared its story, we can explore, with curiosity, whether a retrieval or do-over is needed. This step, whether working with children or adults, is only taken if it aligns with what the client's system needs at that moment. With children, it's important to remember that they may not fully understand these concepts when explained directly. This is where the sandtray becomes a powerful tool, allowing the process to unfold symbolically and in a way that feels natural to the child.

RETRIEVAL AND DO-OVER

During retrieval or do-over work, we must stay attuned to the client's emotional state and narrative, ensuring that any offering or intervention is introduced at the right point in the IFS sandtray process. For example, to facilitate retrieval, we might ask, "Would the miniature like to leave the tray or move to a different space?" For a do-over, we can invite the child to add to the scene by asking, "Can you place something in the tray that shows what the miniature needed right after that happened?" By carefully pacing these interventions and respecting the client's readiness, we help the exile experience safety, care, and the possibility of healing in a way that feels organic and supportive.

In my sandtray work, I've observed that retrieval and do-over often naturally blend together, especially when working with younger children who may not always grasp the difference between taking a target miniature out of a sandtray and adding new, helpful elements that the target miniature may want or need to the sandtray. We can seamlessly combine these processes by offering the child a simple invitation to make any changes the exile needs in that moment. This approach aligns with the principles of child-centered play therapy, reinforcing the belief that children possess the inner resources necessary for healing. It also reflects the core IFS concept that the client's Self is the primary healing agent. By trusting the child's innate ability to guide the process, we create space for organic and meaningful transformation to occur within the sandtray, empowering the child to facilitate their own healing journey.

> **ME:** It must have been really hard for Little Max when he started at the new school. Would you like to change anything about your tray, or does Little Max want to be in a different place?
>
> **CLIENT:** [*adds more people figures in the tray*]
>
> **ME:** Would it be okay if you tell me about what you added to the tray?
>
> **CLIENT:** Little Max wished that more teachers were on the playground and in the classroom. Maybe with more teachers, kids would not be so mean.

UNBURDENING

The unburdening in sandtray work with children often unfolds naturally, as children are inclined to release emotions and beliefs spontaneously through play. When the moment feels right, you can gently ask your client if the part is ready to let go of the heavy emotions or beliefs it has carried from past experiences: "I bet that miniature felt a lot of big feelings, thoughts, and maybe even some funny or uncomfortable things in its body when that happened. Do you think the miniature might be ready to let go of some of those feelings, even just a little bit?" If the part indicates readiness, we invite the child to unload these burdens in whatever way feels comfortable and meaningful to them, using the sandtray as a safe and expressive space. This might involve adding new miniatures or objects that symbolize healing, protection, or strength, or removing items that represent pain, fear, or negative beliefs. This symbolic act of unburdening helps the exile feel lighter and more connected, fostering deeper integration and emotional relief.

Other gentle, child-friendly statements that support unburdening include:

- Does this miniature feel ready to let go of any of the heavy feelings it's been carrying?

- If this miniature could take out the yucky or hard stuff and leave it in the sand, what would it want to take out?

- Is there anything this miniature doesn't need to hold onto anymore? Maybe we can add or move something in the tray to show that.

- What could help this miniature feel lighter or happier? Would it like to place something new in the sand to help with that?

- If this miniature wanted to give away the heavy feelings to the sand or another figure, would that feel okay?

> **ME:** I bet that Little Max felt a lot of big feelings, thoughts, and maybe even some funny or uncomfortable things in his body when on the playground in the classroom. Do you think he might be ready to let go of some of those feelings?
>
> **CLIENT:** Yes he would.
>
> **ME:** Maybe you can add or move something in the tray to show that.
>
> **CLIENT:** [*adds the purple* Inside Out *figure that represents fear in the corner of the tray and puts sand over it*]
>
> **ME:** Would it be okay to share about what just happened?
>
> **CLIENT:** Little Max wanted the fear he was always feeling to go away, so I buried it in the sand for him.

INVITATION

During the sandtray session, you can gently invite your client to connect with the part and explore what positive qualities it might like to welcome in. This could include feelings or strengths the part needs moving forward or qualities that may have been pushed aside by the burdens it carried. You might say something like "I wonder if this miniature wants to bring in anything that could help it feel stronger, happier, or safer?" By offering this invitation, you encourage your client to imagine and symbolize these qualities in the sandtray, perhaps by adding new miniatures or shifting existing ones. This process empowers the child to envision a future where the part feels supported and nurtured, reinforcing the belief that healing is not just about letting go, but also about making space for growth and resilience.

> **ME:** Now that the fear Little Max was always feeling is gone, what positive things would he like to replace it with in the tray?
>
> **CLIENT:** Little Max wants to be braver.
>
> **ME:** Would you like to pick a miniature that represents being brave?
>
> **CLIENT:** [*adds another, different dragon to the tray*]

INTEGRATION

As the sandtray session progresses toward integration, the therapist can guide the child in welcoming the protective parts back into the process. This part of the healing process reinforces the idea that protectors are valuable and have an important role, even after the exile has been unburdened. You might say, "Do you think the miniature that helped protect you wants to come back and see how things are now?" or "I wonder what your protector would like to do now that the other miniature feels better?" This invitation allows the child to reconnect with their protectors in a new way, often leading to a shift in the protector's role from one of defense to one of support. The child may express this by moving the protector figure closer to the exile or placing it in a new position within the tray, symbolizing a harmonious relationship between parts. This integration work helps the system feel more balanced and allows the child to witness how all parts can coexist peacefully, fostering a sense of internal harmony and safety.

> **Me:** I wonder if 8-year-old Max would like to come back and see what Little Max has been up to.
>
> **Client:** Yeah . . . but he's been watching the whole time.
>
> **Me:** Oh wow! Since he's been watching, I wonder how he wants to help Little Max now that he let the fear go and replaced it with bravery?
>
> **Client:** Hmm, maybe not staying away from the other kids and making friends with them?
>
> **Me:** It sounds like 8-year-old Max isn't going to work so hard to keep Little Max away and trust him to be brave.
>
> **Client:** But what if Little Max gets scared?
>
> **Me:** Little Max might get scared, but he has 8-year-old Max to help him be brave and to walk away if he needs to.
>
> **Client:** That sounds really good.

As the sandtray session draws to a close, you can gently invite the child to set an intention to stay connected with the part moving forward. This can help the child build a sense of ongoing care and responsibility for their internal world. The therapist might say, "Do you think you could check in with the miniature sometimes to see how it's feeling?" This simple commitment reinforces the idea that the part is not alone and that the child's Self can continue to provide support. To end the session, the therapist can guide the child in offering appreciation to all the parts that showed up and worked hard during the process: "Can we thank all the miniatures for everything they've done to help?" This moment of gratitude helps solidify the healing experience, acknowledging the important roles each part has played. By fostering appreciation and connection, the therapist supports the child in developing a compassionate relationship with their inner system, reinforcing balance and trust.

> **ME:** I wonder if you could check in on Little Max and 8-year-old Max sometimes to see how they are feeling?
>
> **CLIENT:** Hmm, how can I do that?
>
> **ME:** Just like you connected with them while in here, you can connect with them when you are away from here.
>
> **CLIENT:** Oh yes, I can do that.
>
> **ME:** Can we take a few moments and thank Little Max and 8-year-old Max for all the things they shared with us?
>
> **CLIENT:** Yes, I can do that.

Conclusion

For children and adults alike, sandtray therapy bridges the gap between the conscious and the subconscious, allowing healing to unfold organically at a pace that respects the client's readiness. When words are difficult or inaccessible, the sandtray provides an alternative path to self-discovery. It invites curiosity, imagination, and playfulness, elements that are often essential to disarming protectors and allowing deeper work to take place with miniatures representing parts.

As therapists, our goal is to follow the client's lead, trusting their system to reveal what is needed in each moment. By holding space—in this case, the sandtray—with patience and openness, we support our client in reconnecting with their Self-energy: the true agent of healing. By weaving together the creative expression of sandtray therapy and the transformative principles of IFS, we can offer clients a holistic and deeply personal pathway to healing.

CHAPTER 6

Playful Parts Activities: LEGO

We already know that Playful Parts is a powerful approach to working with children. However, integrating sandtray and other expressive arts activities makes it even more powerful. When I began to use sandtray, LEGO, and other expressive arts with my clients, I saw transformations that were not otherwise accessible.

There are lots of reasons for this. First and most obvious, expressive arts activities are generally associated with fun, not with talk, and not with talk-specific therapy. Clients, especially young clients, usually find the prospect of play a lot more attractive than the more abstract prospect of building trust through conversation or other modalities more familiar to adults. Sandtray, LEGO, and other expressive arts activities do not require conversation to "work." They don't even require language. Yet when our clients can build and play with sandtray and LEGO in creative, nonverbal ways, they nonetheless represent their inner systems. These activities therefore offer clinicians new and different tools for enacting the main methods of Playful Parts: Insight and direct access to build the Self-to-part relationship by utilizing externalization.

Though I often rely on sandtray to facilitate this work, I use LEGO activities just as much. LEGO activities are readily recognizable to most kids—they're a familiar toy that most kids (and adults) are interested in interacting with. For our purposes, however, LEGO offers a critical aid to nonverbal externalization. When a client's protective system is activated, they may not be able to communicate their parts' experiences, at least not verbally. They aren't able to recognize their different parts or how those different parts are showing up for them.

This is often the case when a kid comes into my playroom after having what parents or caregivers report was a bad day at school. I might ask my client to share with me what made the day bad. Often, my client gets very quiet and slowly responds with comments like "I don't know," "Just stuff," or "I don't want to talk about it." LEGO offers an opportunity to shift from unproductive to constructive silence. I might respond to my client's reluctance by offering them a pail of LEGO bricks and an invitation: "Can you use LEGO bricks to show me about your bad day?" Now my child no longer has to verbalize something that they may not have words for. Now they can focus their discomfort on building and showing. Once my client is done building, I can ask questions about what they've created, or I can give them an opportunity to sit with the build and notice what comes up for them when they focus in on it. LEGO helps us to alleviate our client's pressure, discomfort, reluctance, resistance, or level of protection. It offers a kind of play activity that can give form, substance, and voice to their internal parts.

As with sandtray activities, LEGO activities offer a play process that fosters safety and distance, allowing clients to explore their inner world with greater clarity and compassion. It also helps clients to build the Self-to-part relationship. We facilitate this by expressing the 8 Cs, which in turn initiates the IFS flow. For instance, depending on the child's age and the level of protection present, we might express curiosity in a variety of ways. We might:

- Ask our client what they are noticing when they look at their build.

- Ask if they can relate to what is shown in the build.

- Ask if the build or a portion of the build could talk, what it would say?

- Give our client the option to journal their thoughts and feelings (journaling does not have to be writing and can instead be expressed through other art activities).

These choice points provide an opportunity for the client—and the clinician too—to gain information about why different parts protect the client's system in the ways they do. This important context can be therapeutically supportive: It's externalization in action, helping to pave the way to insight or direct access.

Externalization is, of course, critical because it helps our client's protectors to be seen, heard, and understood, leading to embodied exploration that can ultimately help our clients to shift extreme protective patterns, foster cooperation among parts, and promote healing. The tangible and experimental nature of LEGO aligns seamlessly with internal systems work, creating opportunities for deeper connection, flexibility, and growth within the client's internal world and the protective system that structures it.

LEGO in the Therapeutic Playroom

Although LEGO has been used in play therapy for at least 20 years, its introduction seems to have been almost accidental. Clinicians stocked their waiting rooms with toys, and over time, some noticed that their clients with autism spectrum disorder not only gravitated toward LEGO, but spontaneously used it to play out various social situations (LeGoff et al., 2014).

My training as a play therapist made use of this insight, and I learned to use LEGO as a tool for facilitating social skills. This approach is commonly applied in group therapy, where each client in a small group is assigned a specific role, such as builder, supplier, or instructor. The group is then challenged to work together in their roles to construct a LEGO structure. The work requires collaboration, communication, and problem-solving. For example, the designated instructor might describe the steps needed to build, while the designated supplier gathers the necessary pieces, and the builder assembles the structure. The activity encourages participants to practice turn-taking, active listening, and teamwork, providing a safe and engaging environment to develop and strengthen social skills. Through their work together, clients not only create something tangible but also build confidence and a sense of accomplishment in their ability to work with others.

Because of this training—and because I happen to love LEGO with all my heart—LEGO has always been a central part of my playroom. It's also a central part of Playful Parts. It's not just that it's easy to play with, it's also that its sets are informed by worldbuilding that doesn't require the full set to be built. LEGO can help many clients to represent and access their internal systems and explore their different parts. When I work with younger clients, I typically introduce LEGO as an open-ended tool, encouraging them to build anything they like—whether it's a structure, a character, or a scene. I might suggest that they create something that represents how they feel that day or that they build a safe place where they can go when they're upset. I also ask questions like "What does this building or character do?" or "Who lives here?" to gently guide them toward thinking about connections between their creations and their emotions or experiences. This helps many clients begin externalizing their inner worlds in a way that feels natural and non-threatening.

For younger clients who aren't immediately engaged with LEGO, I might frame it as a playful challenge by asking if they can help me build something specific, such as "Can you create a hero to help save the day?" Or I might ask them to help me "solve a LEGO mystery." For some clients, themed sets, like castles or vehicles, provide a structured starting point that feels less overwhelming than starting from scratch. In more atypical cases, such as clients who struggle with focus or who find unstructured play difficult, I may take a more directive approach, asking them to create a character or scenario that we can use to tell a story together. This allows us to co-create a narrative that connects to their feelings or challenges, even if they initially resist free play. Through flexibility and creativity, LEGO can become a versatile tool that adapts to both typical and atypical clients, helping them explore and express their inner worlds in ways that feel safe and accessible.

However, when I work with older clients, I might provide them with an easy introduction to IFS and then say something like "Let's use LEGO to build our protective system." Often, clients will construct walls, fortresses, or shields to represent how they guard themselves from vulnerability. Or they might create figures or objects that symbolize their protective parts, such as a knight, a superhero, or even an impenetrable tower. Their build will not immediately point to solutions, but it will almost always reveal underlying dynamics in their system—highlighting what I need to work on to gain their trust and eventually access their parts, especially their exiles.

Typically, I deepen this conversation by asking my older clients what I have to "battle against" to get to their story. This question often resonates, as it frames their protective mechanisms not as obstacles to therapy but as crucial defenders within their internal world. This approach works especially well for teens and young adults who may feel misunderstood or hesitant to open up, as it gives them a creative and symbolic way to express their inner struggles. By externalizing their system in this way, the process helps pave the way toward direct access and eventual in-sight work, enabling a more collaborative exploration of their parts and their experiences.

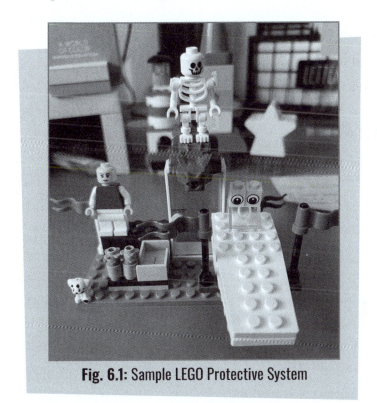

Fig. 6.1: Sample LEGO Protective System

The picture here contains some of my favorite LEGO builds from my work with a client. The first shows the externalization of the protective system and, as such, shows how complex protective systems can be: When my client created this, I gained a deeper understanding of their emotional state and the level of protection they needed before I could access their exiled part.

The skeleton figure at the top that is standing on the alligator symbolizes an ever-present, watchful protective part of the client—a protector that, while intimidating, served as a defense mechanism against perceived threats. Its elevated position reinforced its vigilance and dominance, highlighting how this part was always, in the client's words, "on guard." The client described this figure as the one that "sees everything and makes sure nothing bad happens," revealing its role in keeping them safe, albeit in a rigid and overwhelming way. When exploring this more deeply, the client explained that the skeleton and alligator work together to protect the system by not allowing anyone to get close to the door, which leads to the vulnerable exile or trauma experience. While numerous protectors helped to guard the door, the client also externalized their struggle between wanting to stay safe and wanting to experience more joy and freedom, which in the build was represented by flowers and flags.

Using their build as a point of exploration, I helped the client to reflect on how their protective parts, while well-intentioned, sometimes prevented them from engaging with lighter, more fulfilling aspects of life. The client acknowledged that the dog and the minifigure represented softer, more vulnerable aspects of themselves that felt overshadowed by the skeleton's vigilance. Exploring this dynamic through LEGO enabled the client to see the protective part not as an adversary, but as a part of themselves trying to help, but in a way that could be adjusted. This opened a pathway for us to talk about balance—specifically about how we could appreciate the protector's role while also creating space for connection, creativity, and relaxation. Through this externalization, the client began to explore ways to collaborate with their protective system rather than feeling controlled by it. This, in turn, helped them develop a deeper Self-to-part relationship that allowed more Self-energy to come into the system.

While LEGO is an invaluable source of education for therapists, it can also lead to education and insight for our clients. Most of us don't reflect on the various parts that make up our internal system. We don't think about how they relate to one another or why. When we challenge ourselves to really think about our experiences and the different parts of ourselves that help us to navigate those experiences, we often gain new perspectives on our experiences and ourselves. Similarly, when I ask my client to use LEGO builds to represent their systems, they sometimes learn something new about themselves—their parts and the relationships between and among those parts—in a more tactile way. For me, this is what makes LEGO so suited to Playful Parts and to building the Self-to-part relationship: It allows my client to gain an understanding of their systems and how their protectors serve as the cause of their protective behaviors.

When LEGO activities work to deliver IFS insights, clients also gain practice in establishing space between Self and parts. This is the work of unblending that is so necessary for the internal system to operate harmoniously. Simply using LEGO to build their internal system, and then discussing the correspondence between their builds and the parts that make up that internal system, creates the distance among various parts that constitutes unblending. Using LEGO, clients don't respond *as* protectors; instead, they use LEGO pieces to *represent* protectors, often supplying those protectors with a voice. In this way, clients learn to *tell* their story rather than *be* the story.

While LEGO activities seem to be especially suitable for boys (this is no doubt informed by strong marketing forces), it's really suitable for any child (and often adults too) who struggles to talk about their feelings or who simply has a hard time connecting to or speaking about their stories. It's also suitable for clients who stand to benefit from the visual and tactile representation of their different parts. The activities let our clients build out their world in the ways they see it—and the ways they want to see it.

Serious Play and the Duck Challenge

In Playful Parts, LEGO activities are informed by IFS and by the work of LeGoff and colleagues (2014), who discuss how LEGO-based activities, including the LEGO® SERIOUS PLAY® (LSP) method, can foster social skills in children with autism. The LSP method was developed by the LEGO Group in the mid-1990s. The concept was primarily created by Johan Roos and

Bart Victor, two professors at the International Institute for Management Development in Switzerland. They collaborated with Kjeld Kirk Kristiansen, the former CEO of LEGO, to design a method for using LEGO bricks to facilitate creative thinking, problem-solving, and communication in business and organizational settings with hands-on, three-dimensional modeling. The method has since evolved into a widely used facilitation tool in workshops and team-building exercises (Kristiansen & Rasmussen, 2014). Though it was originally conceived of as a tool for the corporate setting, concepts from LSP are now used in therapeutic and educational settings to enhance communication, self-expression, and the use of metaphors (similar to the use of the sandtray). As a certified facilitator, I've seen firsthand how effective the method can be for fostering problem-solving and team-building in group clinical supervision and direct therapeutic practice.

My favorite way to use the LSP method is the Duck Challenge, though to transform it into a more therapeutic concept, I like to call it the Duck Directive. I typically introduce the Duck Directive to clients though a Meet-the-Duck activity.

MEET THE DUCK (AND DISCOVER PARTS)

In this activity, participants are instructed to use simple—but, of course, highly variable—LEGO bricks to build a duck. The activity assumes that there is no right—or wrong!—way to build a duck. As such, it can serve as an excellent icebreaker and first therapy session activity to start externalizing the internal system. When I playfully challenge my client to build a duck, I build a duck too. After we've both completed our build, we admire and discuss what we've created.

The versatility of the Duck Directive is attributable to the duck's status as a low-stakes, approachable object. In my playroom, its simplicity makes it accessible for clients of all ages and skill levels. A directive like "build a duck" feels a lot more manageable than something like "build your protective system." Consequently, even my most reluctant clients typically feel pretty comfortable engaging with the activity, which is why I use it so often in my work with children and families.

The duck's playful simplicity also facilitates a very broad range of symbolic thinking. For my clients, particularly those who are more hesitant to engage in more abstract work, the duck build, once completed, can represent anything from safety and resilience to challenges or unmet needs. We can explore these in conversation, through questions like "What does this duck need to feel safe?" or "What adventure would this duck go on?" Such questions encourage storytelling and externalization of complex emotions, fostering deeper insight through what (on the surface) looks like a simple duck. Through its unassuming but incredibly versatile nature, the duck serves as a bridge to self-discovery, creativity, and meaningful therapeutic dialogue.

THE DUCK DIRECTIVE

OBJECTIVE: Introduce the client to their parts by projecting them onto a simple LEGO duck.

INSTRUCTIONS:

Fig. 6.2: LEGO Duck

1. Take six LEGO bricks for yourself and provide your client with six LEGO bricks as well.

2. Explain that you'd like to invite them to create a duck. Explain that both of you will build your own versions of a duck. Emphasize that there is no right or wrong way to build their duck and that they should allow the duck to take whatever form they prefer.

3. After building, ask the client the following questions:

   ○ If this duck represents a part of you, which part do you think it might be?

   ○ How does this duck feel today?

4. Encourage the client to name the duck. Examples include *Worried Duck* or *Strong Duck*.

· ·

PLAYFUL PARTS CONNECTION: This exercise allows protectors or exiles to gently surface in a non-threatening way. It bypasses over-analysis by inviting creativity, which often leads to unexpected insights.

This is particularly the case when it intersects with Playful Parts. I think back to a client whose duck represented a protective part—its wings "shielded" other parts, and its small, stable form felt, to the client, grounded and safe. Alternatively, another client used the duck to explore an exile part, giving voice to its vulnerability by removing pieces or altering its structure to reflect their sense of its fragility. By constructing and interacting with the duck, clients can externalize their parts, facilitating discussions about their roles, relationships, and struggles in a way that still can feel safe and playful.

The Duck Directive also provides opportunities to solicit and express Self-energy through the 8 Cs, including connection, creativity, and curiosity—and even courage and compassion as we consider what the duck may have experienced too. In this way, the Duck Directive can also set a strong foundation for reaching bigger goals.

Other LEGO Activities in Action

The Duck Directive is far from the only way to use LEGO to reach Playful Parts goals. In fact, I learn more about the healing potential of different LEGO activities nearly every working day. In this, my work with Adam stands out, as his experience helps illustrate how versatile LEGO can be. Adam came to see me at about 10 years old. His infancy was marked by a premature birth and a failure-to-thrive diagnosis. He was placed for adoption, and at 3 years old, he was adopted by a queer male couple. I met Adam after he began to be bullied at school. His parents realized that Adam's classmates had begun to call him "stupid" and "gay," and Adam's teacher commented that she saw a shift in his behavior within the classroom setting and in Adam's grades. Although Adam had previously made excellent grades and enthusiastically participated in school, as he began to experience more bullying, his grades dropped, and he began to withdraw—both from school and from his parents.

Adam's parents felt immediate concern less because of Adam's "big behaviors" and more because of their personal experiences. They recognized in Adam some of the emotional, behavioral, and physical distress they experienced as children after being abused and bullied. While they wanted to talk with Adam about his feelings and his experiences—and they often asked him about school—Adam refused to engage. Instead, he withdrew into himself, showed less interest in prior activities, and began making attempts to change his appearance.

When Adam's parents found some unexplained bruising, damaged belongings, and missing personal items, they realized they needed more support. They wanted to know how to help Adam and how to handle other seemingly related issues, such as an increase in Adam's daily complaints about headaches, stomachaches, and trouble sleeping. Additionally, Adam had begun to ask if he could stay home from school, while at the same time becoming secretive about his behaviors and interactions at home. Adam's parents hoped that he would feel comfortable talking to someone other than either of them about his experiences at school and changes within the home situation.

My first meetings with Adam confirmed his parents' view: He was withdrawn and didn't seem to want to communicate his feelings at all, nor did he want to consider his parts or their experiences—whether those experiences happened in school or out of it. During the first two sessions, Adam responded minimally to my questions, often giving short, guarded answers or shrugging in silence. At times, he avoided eye contact entirely, retreating into what appeared to me to be his own world, as if to shield himself from any potential vulnerability associated with opening up. His protective behaviors were obvious and signaled a deep reluctance to let his guard down. This, of course, shaped the initial dynamic of our therapeutic work, in part because it indicated a starting point for finding a target part.

I wanted to know what part of Adam was the most activated when he was bullied, but Adam was clearly unable to communicate this. His protectors seemed to be keeping him from sharing their experiences, likely because those parts didn't feel that adults like me were trustworthy. It was as though Adam was saying, "My protectors don't trust you because you haven't really helped me. You aren't going to be able to do anything to stop the bullying anyway."

After our first few sessions, during which I worked in various ways to engage Adam, I sought to communicate to him that I heard what his protectors were saying, even when they weren't saying anything at all. I spoke directly to those protectors, admitting that what Adam suspected about my role was right: I wasn't at his school, and I wouldn't be able to stop the bullying that he was experiencing. I also wouldn't be able to change others' bullying behaviors. I explained this to Adam, and then I also explained that my job was to talk with him and to support him as he thought about what he wanted to do about his situation.

Recognizing Adam's continued hesitation, I made it a priority to create a safe and non-threatening environment where he could begin to trust me, even in small ways, by continuing to speak directly to his protectors. I told Adam that my role wasn't to force him to talk or feel a certain way but to support him in figuring out how to feel more comfortable with himself and also with whatever was going on in his world. I explained that therapy didn't have to be about talking if he didn't want it to be—it could be about doing things that felt easier, like playing with some LEGO bricks or building something together. I reassured him that he could take his time and that I wouldn't pressure him to share until he was ready. With these words, I relied on my own Self-energy as the healing agent—rather than Adam's—to make a meaningful connection to Adam's protectors.

I stayed patient and consistent, meeting Adam where he was and inviting him to work together with me on something fun. Directing his attention to the LEGO bricks, I invited him to choose which pieces we should use to build something "just for fun." The nonverbal, playful approach allowed Adam to engage on his own terms, without feeling interrogated or judged. Gradually, as we sat side by side building together, Adam began to offer small, spontaneous comments about his creations. These moments signaled the start of a connection as he started to test the waters of opening up, even if only a little. Through these small interactions, Adam began to see that I wasn't there to push him but to be a supportive presence he could trust—together, we could just play LEGO.

I saw my initial role with Adam as one of building his trust through a combination of providing consistency, displaying continued patience, and maintaining a focus on creating a safe and inviting space. In this, I paid close attention to Adam's cues, letting him set the pace for all of our interactions, and respecting the nonverbal boundaries that were clearly set by his protective system. Even though the work was slow, I was able to maintain a warm and nonjudgmental demeanor because I continued checking in on *my* parts.

There were parts of me that wanted Adam to do more and say more during the sessions. This is incredibly common—there are parts of all therapists that want our clients to participate more actively or simply with less reluctance. That's why we check in with our own parts, asking them to step back so as to allow more of Self-energy to become present and available for our clients. With Adam, this was especially important because it ensured he felt no pressure to engage with me, or with "the work," beyond his comfort level. The pressure-free environment of the playroom helped foster in Adam a sense of control and safety, especially around his play. It was easy for me to see that this was critical for him, as he clearly didn't feel this way in the school or home setting.

Our early work together proceeded similarly. I offered him choices, such as deciding which activities to do or what materials to use, empowering him to take ownership of our time together. I also mirrored his energy and interests, allowing moments of quiet to exist without rushing to fill them, showing him that I respected his need for space. Using humor and lighthearted comments during play, like "Wow that is soooo cool!" about a particular build, helped break down barriers, making our interactions feel more natural and less formal. Over time, I celebrated even the smallest wins—like when Adam shared a brief thought about his LEGO creation—acknowledging his courage and validating his experiences. By building a predictable routine and showing consistent care and curiosity, I began to earn more of Adam's trust, creating the foundation for deeper exploration when he was ready for it.

I knew the message of safety was getting through to Adam because he began to communicate more with me. As we worked on our builds, he started offering brief explanations about his creations, commenting on a structure ("This is a castle to keep things out") or gesturing to a build ("This one's supposed to look tough"). Additionally, he began to glance at me more and more while building, checking for my reaction to his builds and to his commentary, sometimes even smiling when I commented on his designs. These are small moments of engagement, but they showed that Adam was beginning to feel more comfortable sharing parts of his world, even if only through play.

Adam also began to take small risks in our interactions: As we began to work on builds together, he started to ask for specific LEGO pieces and made playful suggestions such as "Let's make it taller!" This was a new phase in our relationship. Adam was starting to trust me enough to express his own preferences and ideas. He also started lingering a bit longer at the end of sessions, packing up his things more slowly or asking if he could finish a particular project next time, which indicated he was feeling more at ease in the space. One day, he even commented, "I think this is pretty cool" about a structure we built together—a small but significant acknowledgment that he was finding value in our time. These subtle changes marked important milestones in how his protectors were presenting in the office setting, signaling that Adam was beginning to open up and that his protectors were decreasing their vigilance, even if in incremental ways, and building the foundation for deeper communication and exploration.

When I introduced a bin of LEGO minifigures to Adam, his eyes lit up with a mix of curiosity and excitement—a response I hadn't seen before. He immediately began digging through the figures, carefully selecting a few that seemed to stand out to him. At first, he didn't say much, but his focus and energy were clear as he grouped some characters together while setting others aside. After a few moments, he held up a minifigure with a shield and said, "This one looks like a protector." He then chose another figure, a smaller one, and placed it next to the protector, explaining, "This one needs help."

It was a breakthrough moment, as Adam started creating stories about the figures, using them to express dynamics that paralleled his internal experiences. From this point forward, he began to narrate brief interactions between the minifigures, where the protector kept the smaller figure safe or stood guard against a bad-guy figure that Adam had placed off to the side. Without prompting, Adam had found a way to communicate through the minifigures, giving voice to his thoughts and feelings in a way that felt safe and natural for him. His engagement with the figures was playful, but it wasn't *only* playful—it was also deeply symbolic, offering a window into his internal world and signaling his growing readiness to explore and share.

Over a series of productive sessions, Adam returned again and again to the minifigures, particularly to the Batman figure. This little guy was dressed in a black suit with detailed armor-like printing, a bat symbol emblazoned on the chest, and a flowing black cape. The face, which was partially obscured by a pointed mask with sharp bat ears, had two expressions—one side wore a confident smirk and the other a steely, determined glare. Adam seemed fascinated by the duality, often flipping the head to show different sides depending on the scenario he was creating.

Initially, as Adam adopted Batman as his primary figure, he handled it with a sense of caution and deliberation, as though it held a special significance. He would grip it tightly at first, keeping it close to him, and rarely incorporated it into interactions with the other minifigures. Instead, Batman often stood alone, positioned at the edge of the scene or away from other characters, as if observing from a distance. Adam spent a lot of time adjusting the cape and positioning the figure in a strong, upright stance, clearly portraying him as powerful and in control. These early interactions suggested that Batman symbolized something important to Adam—perhaps a protector or an aspirational part of himself that he wasn't ready to fully explore or integrate yet.

Noticing his continued interest in Batman, I saw an opportunity to begin externalizing Adam's parts. I pointed to the minifigure and asked Adam directly, "Who is this? Is this you?"

"It's me sometimes," Adam responded, gripping the figure and turning it over in his hands. He sat quietly for a moment, flipping the figure's head to switch between its two faces, as if weighing his thoughts. Then, he began to remove the cape, carefully sliding it off. He positioned Batman back on the table without the cape, his movements deliberate and precise. As he adjusted the figure's stance, making sure it stood solidly, Adam finally said, "But I'm only really Batman when Batman's not wearing his cape."

His response and actions were thoughtful and showed how deeply he connected to the figure as a representation of himself. The removal of the cape seemed symbolic—perhaps Adam was shedding a layer of protection or pretense to reveal a more vulnerable or authentic version of himself. This small but profound moment opened a door for us to explore Adam's parts further, using Batman as a bridge to understanding how Adam navigated his internal world.

This admission seemed to point toward the parts of Adam that felt disempowered. I wanted to know more about how he viewed this shift between cape-on and cape-off Batman, so I asked him about the differences between the two versions of Batman. Adam paused, considering, and then replied that cape-on Batman was "strong and ready to fight," while cape-off Batman was "just trying to figure things out" and didn't feel as powerful. Adam said, "Without his cape, he's more like . . . normal, just like me, not as special."

As Adam continued to manipulate the figure, it became clear that he saw Batman as a part of himself that had the potential for both strength and vulnerability. He seemed to view cape-off Batman as more grounded, reflecting a side of himself that was perhaps unsure or struggling, while cape-on Batman seemed to represent the version of himself he aspired to be—tough, invincible, and in control. This distinction helped me see that Adam was beginning to externalize his parts through the lens of Batman, allowing him to explore both his empowered and disempowered feelings in a way that felt safe and manageable.

I knew that to support Adam's internal system and help him build resilience, I needed to help him strengthen his connection with his parts so that he could access, or better express, the power he needed to guide his parts through the difficult experience of being bullied. In Playful Parts, as in IFS, the balance of the whole system is crucial because it allows individuals to access a more integrated sense of Self—through which parts can work together rather than be in conflict. This internal harmony helps a person face challenges—like bullying—with greater clarity, strength, and emotion regulation, as they can draw on the support of their more empowered, protective parts while also addressing the vulnerability of their wounded parts. By fostering a collaborative relationship between Adam's parts, I hoped he would gain the inner resources he needed.

Given Adam's interest in Batman and other LEGO minifigures, I began to shape parts work around Batman's cape. At first, I wanted to understand how Adam viewed Batman's cape and how he might use his understanding of the cape's power to support him in and out of school. I asked different versions of questions like "What does Batman feel like when he wears his cape?" "What happens when he takes it off?" and "How does he feel then?" These questions seem simple, but they aren't. They asked Adam to reflect on aspects of himself through the lens of the minifigure, a symbolic representation of his own internal parts. By inquiring about the cape, I was encouraging Adam to explore the differences between his empowered and vulnerable states, which are often difficult to articulate directly.

For Adam, and for many other clients (kids and adults alike), LEGO minifigures can be a safe, external object that helps them begin to understand and express their internal world. It provides a tangible and relatable medium onto which the client can project their feelings, creating an emotional distance from a situation they may feel is inescapable, partly because it's often connected to feelings of shame, fear, and confusion. A minifigure can also allow them to engage with their emotions indirectly, making it easier to approach difficult topics, or making it easier to talk about something that might otherwise feel overwhelming or confusing.

For example, rather than Adam directly saying something like "I feel powerless at school," he can talk about Batman's cape and how it makes Batman—not Adam, necessarily—feel either empowered or vulnerable. This indirect approach opens up conversations that might otherwise be blocked, allowing a client like Adam to gain real insights into their emotions and experiences. Therapist-directed questions like "What does this figure want to do?" or "How does this part of you handle tough situations?" can facilitate exploration of parts that might otherwise stay hidden.

Similarly, when Adam imagined a part of himself as Batman, it gave him the comfort he sought to talk about a challenge that was otherwise too uncomfortably close to discuss. Using LEGO to express his feelings about the cape, Adam was able to explore the parts of him that felt strong and protected (when wearing the cape) and the parts that felt vulnerable or uncertain (when the cape was removed). Discussing this challenge as a familiar scenario from LEGO gave him a language he already knew, which helped him to apply it to his own challenges—especially the ones related to bullying—and to articulate his feelings about those challenges.

For Adam, as for other clients, LEGO provided a bridge between his internal and external worlds, helping give voice to his experiences in a way that felt safe and meaningful. As he gained confidence in the playroom, he began to engage with other expressive arts activities, including the sandtray. He began to create scenarios in which Batman faced a variety of villains, and he began to imagine what it might mean to be courageous or, in the language of LEGO, to "wear a cape like Batman."

Fig. 6.3: Adam's Sandtray

Sandtray and LEGO: A Dynamic Duo

In the sandtray figure shown here, Adam carefully positioned villain figures to create a menacing scene. A character holding a knife was placed in the back corner; a figure with large eyes stood watch over the scene; and a giant owl dominated the center of the tray. The arrangement suggested a deliberate attempt to evoke danger and control. Interestingly, Batman was placed on the tray's far side, though Adam later took Batman out of the tray, keeping the miniature close to him and away from the conflict, away from the sandtray. When I asked Adam about this, he said, "They're always there, watching me" and "They make it so I can't do anything." He also added, "It feels like I'm trapped with them."

At this point, I noticed that Adam was holding Batman and that he had taken off Batman's cape. When I asked Adam about this, he responded, "Without his cape, Batman can't do anything. He's stuck, just like me. But if he had his cape, maybe he could fight back and get in there."

Over the course of several sessions, Adam began to express that he could be more like Batman—and wear his cape—if he were also more like Bruce Wayne and able to "take care of his business." This insight emerged as a collaborative process: I asked Adam what Bruce Wayne does when he's not being Batman, and this prompted Adam to think about the parts of Bruce's life that support his ability to be a hero. Adam started using LEGO to brainstorm what "taking care of business" might mean for him. Piece by piece, he built small structures to represent his schoolwork, homework, and grades, identifying these as his "business." He recognized that, like Bruce Wayne, he needed to handle these responsibilities to feel strong and confident enough to face his own villains.

To help Adam connect this realization to his life outside of therapy, we broke down what "taking care of business" could look like day to day. For example, Adam decided that keeping up with his homework could be one of the ways he practiced wearing his cape. In turn, he built a small LEGO structure to symbolize his "homework headquarters," which he said could remind him to stay on track. Between sessions, his parents reported small but encouraging changes—he started organizing his schoolwork more and even mentioned wanting to "get his Bruce Wayne stuff done" before playing. These small shifts showed how Adam was beginning to internalize the balance between Bruce and Batman, using the idea to prioritize his responsibilities and empower himself to face challenges with a growing sense of agency and strength. The process highlighted how play and creativity could make abstract concepts like responsibility and empowerment tangible and relatable for Adam, helping him connect them to his real-life experiences.

Over time, Adam reported, and his dads confirmed, that rather than withdraw from school, he began to participate again. For instance, his grades came back up, he was selected as student of the month, and he was recognized on the honor roll. He also received a reading award. These victories helped him gain the confidence he sought to "wear the cape" to school. As a consequence, Adam also began to intervene with the bullies in more appropriate ways. He began to report that when the bullies taunted him by calling him "stupid and gay," it didn't bother him as much. He may not have known whether or not he was gay, but "I know I'm not stupid," he told me. This recognition was a strong assertion of Self and Self-energy, and it enabled Adam to feel more ambivalent about their other insults.

Conclusion

In Playful Parts, LEGO offers a powerful, hands-on approach to healing and integration. Through the simplicity of building and storytelling, clients can externalize their inner worlds, giving form to parts that may have felt hidden or voiceless. Each brick and figure becomes a metaphor for the burdens carried by protectors and exiles, while the process of creating, modifying, and unburdening mirrors the transformative journey toward leading with Self-energy. By fostering a playful and safe environment, LEGO bridges the gap between imagination and emotional healing, allowing clients of all ages to reconnect with their core Self. In this space of creativity and compassion, the path to inner harmony becomes not only possible but profoundly engaging and empowering.

On the next pages, you'll find a variety of LEGO-based activities I have used to facilitate Playful Parts in my session with clients. These activities are designed to help clients externalize and engage with their internal parts, fostering self-awareness, compassion, and healing. Importantly, however, they're also a lot of fun! Clients of all ages typically enjoy the playful approach to what may otherwise feel like challenging work.

"REBUILD THE DUCK": TRANSFORMATION AND UNBURDENING

OBJECTIVE: Facilitate the healing and transformation of burdened parts.

INSTRUCTIONS:

1. Ask the client to modify the duck they created in the previous *Duck Directive* activity to reflect how this part carries burdens. For example, they might add extra bricks to make it feel "heavy" or fragile.

2. Explore the burden they've added by asking questions like "What do these extra pieces represent?"

3. Guide the client to remove or rearrange bricks to symbolize the unburdening process by asking questions like:

   ◦ "What can we remove from this duck to help it feel lighter or freer?"

   ◦ "Can we add anything to help this duck feel stronger?"

   ◦ "Can we add anything to the duck or around the duck so it can sit more comfortably or can sit without teetering?"

4. Solicit the client's externalization of and reflection on the unburdening process by asking questions such as:

   ◦ "What does the duck look like now without the burden?"

   ◦ "How does the duck feel lighter or freer?"

   ◦ "What helps the duck stand more comfortably now?"

· ·

PLAYFUL PARTS CONNECTION: This physical transformation mirrors the unburdening process in IFS, helping clients visualize the parts becoming freer after healing.

MAPPING THE INTERNAL SYSTEM

OBJECTIVE: Externalize the client's internal system by creating multiple builds, each representing a different part.

INSTRUCTIONS:

1. Ask the client to create builds to represent different parts of their system. If your client has completed the *Duck Directive*, consider suggesting different ducks for this purpose. Regardless of form, clients should create the following:

   - A build that represents their protector

   - A build that reflects an exile

   - A build that represents the client in the here and now

2. Encourage the client to get creative and ensure each creation reflects the part's qualities. For instance, a protector build might be big and tall to keep others away.

3. Instruct the client to place the different builds in a sandtray or on a table according to how they relate to one another.

4. Facilitate a dialogue between the different builds to learn more about their relationships:

   - "Which parts feel close to each other?"

   - "Which parts stay far apart from one another?"

   - "If they could talk, what would they say?"

   - "How can the here-and-now part comfort the others?"

. . . .

PLAYFUL PARTS CONNECTION: This visual and spatial representation helps clients map relationships between parts, fostering internal balance and compassion.

THE PROTECTOR'S FORTRESS

OBJECTIVE: In this activity, the client can create a build of any kind (including a duck, of course), as long as it represents a protective part and helps them to understand their protective part's role.

INSTRUCTIONS:

1. Ask the client to build a fortress or shield using LEGO bricks to represent a protector part.

2. Use the following questions to learn more about this protector and explore its role in the internal system:

   ◦ "What is this fortress (or shield) protecting?"

   ◦ "How strong is it?"

   ◦ "If this fortress (or shield) could speak, what would it say about the part it's protecting?"

3. Have the client build a small figure or object to symbolize the exile hidden inside or behind the fortress (or shield).

4. Engage in dialogue between the fortress and the exile.

   ◦ "Is there anything that the fortress wants to say to the exile?"

   ◦ "What does the exile want the fortress to know?"

. . . .

PLAYFUL PARTS CONNECTION: The symbolism of the LEGO figures reveals the burden of the protector and the vulnerability of the exile, fostering empathy and connection between the two.

THE GUARDIAN AND THE EXILE

OBJECTIVE: Help clients uncover exiles that are hidden behind protector parts.

INSTRUCTIONS:

1. Ask the client to build a guardian (protector) using LEGO bricks, making it as strong or elaborate as they like. This build may be as basic as a wall of bricks or as complex as a large robot.

2. Ask the client to build a small fragile figure, representing the exile, to place behind the guardian. This build may be as simple as the client placing one brick behind their protective build.

3. Explore the relationship between the two:

    ◦ "Why does the guardian feel it needs to protect this exile?"

    ◦ "What would happen if the guardian did not do its job?"

. . . .

PLAYFUL PARTS CONNECTION: Similar to *The Protector's Fortress* activity, this visual and spatial representation helps externalize the parts' relationships, creating separation between the protector and exile, and opening the door for healing through the Self.

THE BRIDGE OF CONNECTION

OBJECTIVE: Create channels for communication and foster harmony between polarized parts that are in conflict with one another.

INSTRUCTIONS:

1. Ask the client to build two LEGO figures representing parts that struggle to communicate with each other (e.g., a harsh inner critic and a vulnerable little one).

2. Ask the client to build a bridge or pathway between the two figures.

3. Use metacommunication to gain more information by asking explicit questions about the build. For example, acknowledge the distance between the two builds: "There is a short path from the anger part and the little one. Are they close to each other?"

4. Facilitate a conversation with the client to gain more information on how the client views the bridge and the connection represented by the bridge. The conversation also aids the client's externalization, in part by allowing the client to represent different possibilities for the bridge.

   - "What does the bridge represent for you?"

   - "What does this bridge represent for the two parts present?"

   - "What would it take for these two parts to meet in the middle?"

5. Encourage the client to represent different ways the parts could meet in the middle by adding or removing bricks to the bridge.

   - If the client removes bricks and allows the two parts to get close, this can represent trust between the two parts, showing that the client is ready for the two parts to be in connection with each other.

   - Alternatively, the client may add bricks or move the figures further away from one another. This may indicate that the child requires more work with protectors to help clear the way for the expression of Self-energy.

· ·

PLAYFUL PARTS CONNECTION: This activity encourages clients to experiment with different approaches to altering relationships among parts. Ideally, clients will bring polarized parts into harmony, but this depends on the client's Self-energy and trust in their ability to facilitate a positive relationship with their parts.

"THE LONG JOURNEY": NARRATIVE BUILDING

OBJECTIVE: Use storytelling to explore part narratives and shift them toward healing.

INSTRUCTIONS:

1. Invite the client to build a figure (maybe a duck!) that represents themselves. Then, invite the client to imagine that their figure is going on a long or difficult journey to a wonderful place.

2. Ask the client to build obstacles (using LEGO bricks) for their figure to encounter. (If your client struggles to build obstacles, offer suggestions such as walls of varying heights, no-trespassing signs, or fences.)

3. Ask the client to guide their figure on the journey, narrating the obstacles their figure encounters and the different ways it can overcome them. Prompt their narrative with questions like:

   ○ "What challenge does the figure face?"

   ○ "What makes this obstacle a challenge for the figure?"

   ○ "How can the figure overcome this obstacle?"

   ○ "Can someone or something help the figure overcome this obstacle?"

4. When the figure overcomes an obstacle, encourage the client to add bricks or modify the figure in some way to represent what the figure has gained or learned from overcoming the obstacle.

. . . .

PLAYFUL PARTS CONNECTION: This exercise draws out the parts' hidden narratives. The story allows the client to witness parts moving from fear to empowerment through the symbolic journey of a figure that grows and learns after overcoming obstacles.

STRENGTHENING THE SELF

OBJECTIVE: Reinforce the role of the Self in guiding and nurturing parts.

INSTRUCTIONS:

1. Have the client create a new build that represents their calm, compassionate Self. (If your client struggles with this task, remind them that their build can take any shape they like, including a duck, if that's a familiar build from the previous activity.)

2. Place this Self-figure next to any previously built figures, such as those from *Mapping the Internal System* activity.

3. To better understand the client's sense of their Self's relationships to their parts, encourage them to narrate the Self-figure's sense of it in comparison to any other figures. Ask questions such as:

   - "What is the Self-figure like?"
   - "How is the Self-figure the same as the other figures?"
   - "How is the Self-figure different?"
   - "How does the Self-figure want to help the other figures?"
   - "What message does the Self-figure have for the other figures?"

- -

PLAYFUL PARTS CONNECTION: This visualization strengthens Self-leadership by creating a nurturing external representation of the client's core Self. This allows the child to have an experience with Self.

CHAPTER 7

Other Expressive Arts Activities for Playful Parts

Sandtray and LEGO-based Play Therapy activities are a vibrant and essential part of my playroom, but they're far from the only expressive therapy techniques I use. While sandtray and LEGO can often feel like the star of the show, I incorporate a variety of expressive art activities that offer clients equally powerful avenues for self-exploration and healing. Some of my most cherished tools for externalization and creative engagement include pastel drawing, intuitive drawing, glitter jars, expressive worksheets, and kintsugi pottery. Each of these activities serves as a gateway for clients to externalize their internal experiences, inviting them to interact with their parts in a meaningful and tangible way.

In Playful Parts, the IFS-informed goal is to help clients build a compassionate relationship with their internal parts, allowing Self-energy to emerge and lead the healing process. Expressive art activities align beautifully with this approach, offering clients a nonverbal, creative method to give voice and form to their parts. By transforming inner experiences into external representations, clients can deepen their self-awareness, reduce overwhelm, and foster a more harmonious internal dialogue.

The tools I incorporate are not supplementary; they actively facilitate the exploration of a client's internal system. When clients create pastel drawings or construct glitter jars, they're engaging in an intuitive process that bypasses cognitive defenses and taps into their subconscious (Malchiodi, 2003). This can reveal hidden parts, emotions, and beliefs that might not surface through traditional talk therapy alone. Kintsugi pottery, for example, mirrors the IFS philosophy of embracing imperfection and valuing the beauty in brokenness, reinforcing the message that healing involves honoring each part of the self, including those that have felt fractured or unworthy.

Of course, expressive approaches rooted in play therapy often deviate from the structured steps of the traditional IFS model. But healing is rarely linear. Creativity thrives in fluidity, and the spontaneity of expressive activities allows clients to organically access and engage with Self-energy. In these moments, qualities like curiosity, compassion, and playfulness emerge naturally, setting the stage for profound healing experiences.

While credentialed art therapists and expressive arts therapists offer specialized expertise, the activities presented in this chapter can be effectively integrated as part of the Playful Parts approach without formal art therapy certifications. The focus is not on producing aesthetically pleasing art but on facilitating a process where clients feel safe to explore, express, and externalize their inner world. These tools are adaptable and accessible, making them valuable assets for any play therapist seeking to enrich their practice through expressive techniques.

In the following sections, I provide detailed insights into how I implement each of these expressive activities, highlighting their therapeutic benefits and practical applications. I also discuss how these creative methods naturally align with and enhance the IFS framework, reinforcing the transformative potential of Playful Parts in fostering healing and self-discovery.

Pastel and Intuitive Drawing in Playful Parts

The difference between pastel drawing and intuitive drawing comes down to the materials used and the approach to creating art. Pastel drawing uses soft pastel sticks, which creates smooth, blendable colors. This softness helps connect with more vulnerable parts of the Self, making it a useful tool for working with exiles—the parts that hold pain, fear, or sadness (Malchiodi, 2003). The gentle nature of pastels can encourage these tender parts to express themselves in a safe and nurturing way.

On the other hand, intuitive drawing focuses on spontaneous, emotional expression and can be done with a variety of harder materials like crayons, markers, or pencils. I have recognized in practice that these materials are often better suited for working with protectors—the parts that are more guarded or defensive, or that take on roles to protect the Self from harm. The firmer texture of these mediums can reflect the strength and boundaries protectors often hold, allowing them to express their energy clearly and directly.

While pastel drawing can help bring out softer, hidden parts, intuitive drawing with stronger materials can give voice to protective parts that need to be seen and heard. Both approaches create opportunities for deeper self-exploration and healing, offering a way to engage with different parts through art.

PASTEL DRAWING

In my practice, I often use pastel drawing as a tool for self-expression and exploration. I invite my clients to sit alongside me, each of us using pastels to create an image. This shared activity establishes a sense of partnership and reduces any pressure they may feel. I begin by opening a conversation about how art can serve as a voice for parts of ourselves or our experiences—both positive and challenging. I emphasize that the process is not about creating something perfect but about allowing feelings or different parts to emerge on the page naturally. Clients are encouraged to focus on a specific part of themselves they wish to explore and allow that part to "draw itself." This approach allows clients to access emotions and thoughts that may be difficult to articulate verbally. The act of drawing can bypass the analytical mind, offering insight into inner experiences that might otherwise remain hidden.

Symbolism and Application

The imagery created through pastel drawing often reveals powerful symbols and metaphors that reflect the client's inner world. The soft shapes can embody the emotional landscape of different vulnerable and younger parts.

Colors and patterns become visual representations of emotions, roles, and states of being. For example, soft, flowing shapes may represent nurturing or vulnerable parts. These images offer a tangible starting point for further dialogue, allowing clients to engage more deeply with their inner experiences (Hinz, 2020).

Client Example

Maya, a 15-year-old client, sat cross-legged in the playroom in silence. After working through the 6 Fs of the IFS-informed Playful Parts process, she developed a deep awareness of her system and was ready to engage in the healing steps. I invited her to use the pastels to create an image that could represent her the younger and vulnerable part of her. Through her work with her protective system, she was able to identify the part she had come to know as the source of her quiet sadness.

With a soft sigh, Maya selected light blues and purples, blending them carefully into the shape of a small figure in the center of the page. As she worked, she spoke softly, describing how this part had carried loneliness and fear for a long time. "She's been waiting to be seen," Maya said, adding delicate golden lines around the figure, almost like rays of light.

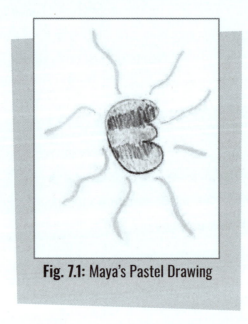

Fig. 7.1: Maya's Pastel Drawing

When the drawing felt complete, Maya paused and gently placed her hand over the image. "I think she's ready to trust me now," she said, her voice steady. Through the act of drawing, Maya created a meaningful connection with her exile, honoring its presence while signaling that healing was underway. After engaging in the pastel drawing activity Maya continued to move forward with telling the story of her younger exile part.

Why Pastel Drawing Works

For clients like Maya, who have gained the trust of their protective system and are ready to engage with more vulnerable parts of themselves, pastel drawing can be a powerful tool. The softness and blendable nature of pastels create a gentle and nurturing medium, making it easier for exiles to safely emerge. This approach is particularly beneficial for individuals who find verbal communication challenging, as it allows them to express emotions and experiences nonverbally. Clients processing trauma or difficult emotions often discover that pastels provide a soothing way to externalize their inner world.

Pastel drawing is effective because it engages the brain's creative and emotional centers, allowing for a holistic and embodied expression of experiences. The soft, tactile nature of pastels can be particularly grounding, creating a safe and gentle way to externalize feelings that may feel too overwhelming to express through words. This makes pastel drawing especially valuable for working with exiles—the vulnerable, wounded parts of the self that often carry feelings of pain, sadness, or fear. The fluidity and blendability of pastels mirror the tender and delicate nature of younger parts, offering a non-threatening way for them to emerge and be seen Rubin, 2016).

By inviting these younger, more fragile parts to express themselves through color and form, clients can begin to witness and build relationships with exiles without the interference of protective parts. The use of pastels can facilitate emotional release and insight, allowing clients to honor their exiles' stories with softness and care. This process nurtures self-compassion by creating a space where all parts are accepted and valued, free from judgment.

Ultimately, pastel drawing opens the door for deeper exploration and transformation, fostering a compassionate dialogue between protectors and exiles. This creative process helps clients integrate their inner worlds, leading to greater self-awareness, connection, and healing.

INTUITIVE DRAWING

Intuitive drawing, which I've already lightly described, is a versatile and accessible tool that I typically use when helping clients engage with their protectors. This activity invites clients to release expectations and allow the marker or crayon to move freely across the page, guided by instinct rather than a specific plan. I encourage clients to choose colors that resonate with them in the moment, fostering a sense of connection and openness. It's a simple but powerful exercise that can soften protective parts, creating space for deeper work with exiles or other less verbal parts. By letting go of any need to create something perfect, clients experience a greater sense of freedom, making it easier for protectors to relax and trust the process. This nonverbal approach is especially helpful for individuals who find it challenging to articulate their experiences or who are drawn to abstract, exploratory methods of parts work.

Symbolism and Application

Like pastel drawing, intuitive drawing often leads to rich symbolic imagery that reflects the client's inner world. Shapes, colors, and movement patterns on the paper can reveal insights about the roles protectors play and the emotions they guard. The act of externalizing these symbols helps clients interact with their parts in a tangible way, fostering understanding and compassion. This activity blends creativity with therapeutic exploration, allowing clients to access deeper layers of their psyche through play and expression (Hinz, 2020).

Client Example

Josh was a 12-year-old client who was new to therapy and was working through the loss of his father. One of the initial goals of our work was to introduce him to the IFS aspect of Playful Parts in an experiential way, focusing on parts mapping to help him identify and understand the different parts of his internal system. During one session, Josh engaged in intuitive drawing using markers as a way to begin identifying and mapping his parts.

Josh's drawing featured dark clouds, which he identified as representations of his protective parts. As we reflected on his artwork, he explained that the dark clouds symbolized the parts of him that prevent him from expressing emotions. Josh shared that his father had instilled the belief that boys don't cry, reinforcing the role of these protective parts in suppressing his feelings. Josh began to recognize that he had different parts within him, marking an important step in his understanding of his internal system. The realization opened space for further exploration of his internal system, allowing for a gentle and supportive introduction to the concept of protectors and exiles.

Because of his comfort with the activity, Josh's ongoing therapy sessions included intuitive drawing as a tool for parts mapping, facilitating dialogue with his protective parts to build trust, and helping them understand their role in his healing.

Fig. 7.2: Josh's Intuitive Drawing

Why Intuitive Drawing Works

Clients who are new to Playful Parts or to other IFS-based therapy can greatly benefit from intuitive drawing as a starting point to explore their protective systems. This creative, nonverbal approach can be particularly helpful for clients who hold strong beliefs that therapy is unsafe or who experience trust issues with adults. Intuitive drawing offers a gentle, less intrusive way to engage with the therapeutic process, making it easier for clients to express themselves without the pressure of more direct, more verbal communication. By engaging the brain's creative and emotional centers, clients can bypass analytical thought and access their internal experiences in a more holistic way. This is partly due to its unrestricted nature, which typically allows and even encourages clients to move and create without judgment, fostering self-compassion and providing a safe space for protective parts to express themselves.

Additionally, as with Josh's engagement, intuitive drawing can be used as a parts-mapping tool to explore various parts of the internal system and help clients visually identify and connect with different aspects of themselves. This can facilitate the discovery of a target part and can also initiate the 6 Fs process with protective parts.

Glitter Bottles in Playful Parts

Glitter bottles are another essential tool in my Playful Parts approach practice. They offer a hands-on, engaging way to help clients of all ages—including adults—navigate overwhelming emotions and reconnect with their own sense of calm. Together with the client, I guide the process of creating a glitter bottle by combining water, glue, glitter, and sometimes additional elements like beads or small objects that can be put in water, inside a clear bottle. This collaborative activity allows clients to engage creatively while building a resource they can use beyond the session.

SYMBOLISM AND APPLICATION

As we mix the materials, I explain the symbolism behind the swirling glitter. The swirling glitter represents the busy, often chaotic nature of thoughts, emotions, and protector parts that arise during moments of stress or emotional activation. The act of shaking the bottle reflects the intensity of these moments, while watching the glitter slowly settle to the bottom of the bottle illustrates the transition from internal unrest to calm, reflecting the capacity to return to a centered, more regulated state. Glitter bottles highlight the idea that our inner system is composed of many parts, and that activation or chaos is a normal part of the healing journey—even just a little bump or a little shake can send glitter spinning.

For younger clients, the glitter bottle serves as a concrete, visual representation and experience of Self-energy, especially calm and clarity. Older clients can engage with the metaphor more abstractly, visualizing and connecting with the experience of observing their parts from a distance and noticing the healing power of Self-energy. Finally, the bottles also offer an opportunity to focus on the 8 Cs of Self-energy, especially to reinforce the reality that Self-energy is not only always present but that it's accessible in moments of activation. Clients learn to cultivate these qualities by using the glitter bottle as a calming tool, facilitating deeper internal alignment and connection to their parts.

CLIENT EXAMPLE

Matthew, 10 years old, often entered the playroom with noticeable tension in his body and a reluctance to engage. He carried significant anxiety, largely stemming from the pressure his parents placed on him to excel academically. Matthew frequently expressed feeling overwhelmed and fearful of disappointing his parents. His protector parts showed up as perfectionism and self-criticism, creating a cycle of stress and internal conflict.

In one session, I introduced the idea of making a glitter bottle as a way to externalize and explore these overwhelming feelings. Matthew was curious but hesitant, a tendency that often manifested in him second-guessing himself. However, as we began crafting the bottle, Matthew became more engaged. I invited him to choose colors and materials that felt right to him. He selected blue and gold glitter, explaining that blue made him feel calm, while the gold reminded him of "winning" and "making people proud."

As we poured the materials into the bottle, I gently introduced parts concepts, explaining how sometimes different parts of us try to help by working really hard, like the glitter swirling when we shake the bottle. I asked Matthew if any parts of him felt like they were always swirling and working. He immediately identified what he called his "school part," which he described as a voice that constantly told him to study more and avoid mistakes. I validated this part's effort to protect him from failure and disappointment, emphasizing that it wasn't bad but rather doing its best to help him. Matthew nodded, quietly adding that this part "never stops." I then invited him to watch the glitter settle, explaining that just like the glitter, his school part could take breaks and allow other parts of him to feel calm and clear.

Over time, Matthew began using his glitter bottle at home when he felt overwhelmed by homework or before tests. In follow-up sessions, he reported that watching the glitter settle helped him feel "less tight" and made it easier for him to focus. This practice supported Matthew in accessing his Self-energy—the calm, compassionate part of him that could appreciate his effort without fear of failure.

The glitter bottle became a tool through which Matthew developed greater awareness of his parts. As he continued working through Playful Parts and using his glitter bottle, he grew more connected to his Self-energy, fostering resilience and reducing the intensity of his perfectionistic protector parts. His parents noted a shift in his demeanor, describing him as "more relaxed" and, over time, less hesitant—or in their words "less afraid to make mistakes."

Fig. 7.3: Matthew's Glitter Bottle

WHY GLITTER BOTTLES WORK

Matthew's experience is reflected in many of my other clients. Regardless of age or the reason for their clinical visits, all clients benefit from the use of glitter bottles. Kids find the process of making and using them fun and engaging, and the tangible nature of the bottle makes complex emotional concepts more accessible. Meanwhile, adolescents and adults use the bottles as a meditative or grounding tool, reinforcing the importance of observation, patience, and acceptance in their healing process.

Glitter bottles are particularly helpful for individuals who struggle with emotion regulation, anxiety, or overwhelming protector parts. These clients may experience rapid shifts in mood or difficulty calming down after parts are activated. Watching the glitter settle is a timed soothing experience that mirrors the internal process of accessing calm and clarity. Additionally, glitter bottles are beneficial for clients working through trauma, as they foster a sense of safety and predictability. Clients can return to the bottle as often as needed, reinforcing their connection to Self-energy and building internal resources for managing stress and anxiety.

The effectiveness of glitter bottles lies in their ability to provide a sensory and visual anchor during moments of emotion dysregulation. The act of shaking the bottle and observing the settling glitter creates a simple, yet powerful, mindfulness practice. This process engages the body and mind, offering a structured way to slow down, regulate the heartbeat, and calm overwhelming thoughts. From a neurological perspective, engaging in a repetitive and predictable activity, such as watching glitter settle, activates the parasympathetic nervous system, promoting relaxation and reducing stress. This supports clients in accessing their Self-energy, reinforcing the notion that they have internal resources to manage difficult emotions and experiences.

Perhaps most importantly, however, glitter bottles also embody the principle that emotions are temporary. By observing the swirling glitter gradually settle, clients internalize the understanding that emotional intensity, like the glitter storm, will pass with time.

Parts of Me Activity in Playful Parts

The *Parts of Me* activity is a versatile part-mapping tool that I integrate into multiple aspects of therapy. It involves using a simple body diagram to have clients identify where and around their bodies they experience their parts. One of the primary ways I use it is to introduce clients to their external system and familiarize them with the concept of parts. This visual approach is particularly effective with clients who are new to therapy or just beginning with the Playful Parts approach. For clients who have been in therapy for a longer period, I use the activity as a means of transitioning them to parts work, creating a pathway for deeper self-exploration. Additionally, the activity is essential when integrating Playful Parts with other therapeutic models such as EMDR. For example, in cases where clients experience stuck points during EMDR, an exploration of their protective parts that might be blocking progress often leads to breakthroughs.

Another way I use the *Parts of Me* activity is as a check-in tool at the start of therapy sessions. Depending on the client's needs, this can serve two distinct purposes: First, the worksheet that accompanies this activity can be used for parts mapping, allowing clients to reflect on the parts that are present and might require attention (see the resource section at the end of this chapter for copies of the worksheet). Alternatively, it can help track which parts surface in and around the body during the retelling of experiences, allowing for somatic engagement. By inviting clients to identify where parts show up in or around the body, the activity fosters a deeper somatic and experiential connection. This process encourages clients to recognize body sensations and express these experiences creatively through words or colors.

The *Parts of Me* activity is adaptable and can also be assigned as homework or a journaling activity. However, I suggest this with caution. It's important to ensure your client's entire system consents to completing homework, as certain parts might resist this, or there may be safety concerns regarding the worksheet's presence outside the therapeutic environment. Typically, these worksheets remain within the therapy setting and are stored in your client's file

SYMBOLISM AND APPLICATION

The symbolism embedded within the *Parts of Me* activity reflects the multiplicity of the human experience. Each part a client identifies represents a facet of their internal world, symbolizing emotions, memories, and protective mechanisms. The act of externalizing these parts through creative expression helps demystify complex internal dynamics. Clients often feel empowered to use colors, shapes, and descriptive language, reinforcing the understanding that no part is wrong or bad.

Moreover, the activity makes tangible our foundational belief every part serves a protective or survival role, even those that might seem disruptive or maladaptive. Through symbolism, clients can begin to appreciate the unique purpose of each part, fostering self-compassion and curiosity. The activity's adaptability allows it to represent the client's external or internal experiences, depending on what feels most resonant at the moment.

CLIENT EXAMPLE

After a year of talk therapy, 10-year-old Sarah remained stuck, struggling to process her feelings and experiences despite numerous interventions. I noticed recurring themes of anxiety and avoidance but was met with resistance whenever I attempted deeper emotional work. To address this, I introduced the *Parts of Me* activity to help Sarah to externalize and identify different parts of herself. During the session, I invited Sarah to draw or color different parts of her that showed up during school or at home. I gave her one worksheet that represented her home parts and one that represented her school parts. She immediately identified a "worried" part that appeared before tests and an "angry" part that emerged during arguments with her siblings at home. By creating visual representations of these parts, Sarah began to engage with the concept of her internal system in a safe and approachable way, fostering her curiosity and reducing her resistance.

Fig. 7.4: Parts of Me A | Parts of Me B

Over time, Sarah's engagement deepened as she grew more comfortable recognizing and naming the different parts of her internal world. I used the activity at the start of each session as a check-in tool, allowing her to reflect on which parts were most present that day. This process gradually unveiled protective parts that previously blocked her from accessing vulnerable emotions, such as sadness or fear. With this new awareness, Sarah became more open to exploring the underlying experiences driving her reactions. By externalizing her parts, she developed a sense of self-compassion and began to lead from a place of greater self-understanding, ultimately unlocking areas where she once felt stuck.

WHY THE PARTS OF ME ACTIVITY WORKS

The *Parts of Me* activity benefits a wide range of clients across different therapeutic contexts. New clients gain an accessible entry point into IFS and parts work, while long-term clients deepen their existing understanding of internal dynamics or, like Sarah, overcome stuck points. The activity is particularly valuable for individuals who experience dissociation, internal conflict, or difficulty accessing emotions because it offers a medium and a method for identifying (mapping different parts), externalizing (enabling the representation of the interior experiences of the parts), and integrating (bringing the parts into a connected, harmonious relationship with another through the mediating Self). It's also beneficial for families, who can engage in this activity together and gain insight into each member's internal experiences. Finally, therapists reap rewards from using this activity as well. The information gleaned through the *Parts of Me* worksheet can provide a roadmap for therapy sessions, ensuring that interventions are precisely tailored to the client's current needs.

The effectiveness of this activity lies in its ability to externalize the internal and in the structured encouragement it offers clients to visualize and name their parts. Like my favorite Playful Parts expressive activities, the *Parts of Me* activity meets clients exactly where they are. Whether used as a brief check-in tool or as part of a more in-depth exploration, it accommodates the fluid and evolving nature of the therapeutic process.

The adaptability ensures that the activity remains relevant across different stages of the client's healing journey.

Kintsugi in Playful Parts*

I love all my Playful Parts tools, but kintsugi, like sandtray and LEGO, is one of my very favorite expressive activities, as it serves as a striking therapeutic metaphor for resilience, transformation, and self-acceptance. Rooted in Japanese art, kintsugi—meaning "golden repair"—is the practice of mending broken pottery by filling the cracks with gold, highlighting the beauty of imperfection and the significance of healing (Kemske, 2021). While it has gained some recognition in the United States, it remains relatively uncommon in therapeutic settings. Yet it aligns seamlessly with Playful Parts—and because it embraces the metaphor of repair, it is especially useful for clients working through shame or trauma. It is also a way to symbolize growth—acknowledging past wounds while celebrating the strength and beauty that emerge from the journey of overcoming adversity. Through kintsugi, clients can reframe their experiences in a more compassionate and empowering way.

Clients can experience kintsugi as a hands-on activity or as a guiding metaphor throughout their healing process—or both! Adaptations might include repairing broken tiles, creating paper mosaics, or gluing ceramic fragments together and accentuating the cracks with gold or metallic paint. These simplified exercises allow clients to physically engage in the act of "mending," offering a tangible reflection of their personal path to healing.

When I guide clients through the kintsugi process, it typically unfolds over multiple sessions, tailored to align with each client's internal system and pace. I begin by introducing the philosophy behind kintsugi, explaining that brokenness does not signify an end but rather a gateway to transformation and beauty. This sets the foundation for clients to understand

---

* I'd like to thank Christa Brennan and her Broken Bowl® workshop for introducing me to the healing potential of kintsugi activities.

how the process mirrors healing, encouraging them to reflect on their own imperfections and experiences.

The journey starts with a simple white ceramic bowl, which I place inside a plastic bag (a practical necessity for containing the fragments but also a symbolic choice because it clearly preserves the entirety of what is about to be broken). Next, I invite the client to break the bowl using a hammer, framing this as a significant ceremony. During this "breaking bowl" ritual, clients are encouraged to turn inward, connecting with their internal system and the bowl as a representation of them as a whole. This stage can evoke powerful emotions, and clients often release feelings tied to their understanding of their brokenness (Hori, 2022).

Following the breaking, we take time to process the experience. I invite them to share any sensations, emotions, or thoughts that surfaced during the activity, fostering reflection on deeply held beliefs about themselves. Clients frequently uncover narratives of instability, self-doubt, or feeling overwhelmed by their emotions—sometimes describing their sense that they are fundamentally broken.

Kintsugi is a practice I like to use with teenagers, but the metaphor can be used with younger clients as well, always with focus on safety. When explaining the kintsugi concept to younger clients, I like to use the phrase "sometimes things break." For instance, I might say, "Sometimes, things break. A favorite toy, a special cup, or even a heart that feels hurt. When something breaks, it can feel sad or scary—like it will never be the same again. But did you know there is a way to fix broken things that makes them even more special than before?"

I remember one of my little clients looking excited at this and saying to me, "I want to learn how to fix broken things." I then said something on the lines of "In Japan, there's a special way to fix broken things called kintsugi, which means golden repair. Instead of trying to hide the cracks when a bowl or cup breaks, we can glue the pieces back together with shiny gold! The gold fills in the cracks, and instead of making the bowl weaker, it makes it stronger and even more beautiful than before. It's like turning something broken into something extra special."

When talking about this with young clients, I like to give them more context that they can relate to by explaining that we sometimes feel like we are broken, just like the bowls in kintsugi. Maybe something happened that made us feel sad, angry, or scared. Maybe we don't feel as strong as we used to. But just like the bowls, we can put our broken pieces back together in a new and special way.

We then proceed to the first step of the kintsugi activity, the breaking of the bowl. This can be done by the client, if they're old enough to safely do so. Or, in the case of a younger client, I will break the bowl according to the client's verbal directions so that they can take an active role in the process. While we break the bowl, I remind them that just because something is broken does not mean it's ruined; it just needs some care to become whole again. I then invite the child to think of a time when they have felt broken or hurt.

During the second step, I help my client to carefully lay out all the broken pieces, inviting them to look at them carefully. Next, I ask, "What do you notice about these pieces?" They might say that some of the pieces are pointy or jagged, while others are smooth and rounded. I affirm that the pieces are all different and then ask, "I wonder if they can still fit together?" This moment helps affirm for clients that even when something is broken, the pieces are still there and coming together again is still possible.

In the third step, clients personalize the broken pieces, which can involve painting, drawing, or writing words and symbols onto the pieces that hold significance for them. This creative process allows clients to project aspects of their identity and life story onto the fragments, fostering deeper connection and meaning. Over time, the broken pieces begin to represent different parts of the client's internal landscape, much like miniatures in a sandtray session. For example, big pieces might represent big events in their lives or their protective parts, and smaller pieces might represent their responses to the big events or their emotions.

Next comes the special part of putting the pieces back together. Instead of using regular glue to put the pieces back together, we use gold paint mixed in the glue to highlight this part of the work. I like to maintain the metaphor by telling my clients that the gold and glue are like kindness and love—it helps us heal when we feel broken inside. I also often reference helpers and the safe adults in the client's life by saying, "I am like the glue and gold, helping you get stronger from an experience that may have caused you hurt."

The process of reassembling the bowl then unfolds gradually, reflecting the client's unique system and needs. For some, this may span three sessions—beginning with the breaking and initial processing, followed by decorating the pieces, and concluding with repairing the bowl. Others may engage in a more extended exploration, dedicating several sessions to understanding and interacting with the broken parts before moving into the repair phase. While some children, including 8- and 9-year-olds, adolescents, teenagers, young people, and adults, are able to take on the majority of this process on their own, younger children will likely require more hands-on support. In these cases, I invite the client to paint some of the pieces as I hold them, and I put the pieces back together, perhaps inviting the client to help me hold pieces together as the glue dries. Regardless, we carefully glue the bowl back together, highlighting the cracks with gold or metallic paint to symbolize resilience and the beauty found in imperfection. As the bowl transforms, so too does the client's relationship with their story—turning perceived brokenness into a source of strength and meaning.

SYMBOLISM AND APPLICATION

It's easy to see how kintsugi serves as a profound metaphor for healing and transformation in Playful Parts. As an expressive arts activity, kintsugi offers a tangible way for clients to externalize and engage with the parts of themselves that have experienced fragmentation. As a therapeutic activity, kintsugi highlights our focus—our work isn't about the trauma or the breaking itself. It's about the parts and the Self that repairs and holds them. Similarly, the art of kintsugi lies not in the breaking of the pottery but in the beautiful work of mending. This gentle reframing invites clients to shift their attention from the intensity of their wounds to the organic need for repair, growth, and integration. To foster conversation and processing while supporting the client on gluing their pieces together, I might ask:

- What do you think the gold means for you?

- Has there been a time when you felt broken but someone helped you feel strong again?

- What would you say to someone else who feels like they have cracks?

Kintsugi also offers clients the opportunity to view their brokenness as a testament to their resilience and capacity for renewal. The repaired vessel tells a story of survival, adaptation, and creativity, reinforcing our belief that healing leads to greater harmony and balance within the internal system. The gold seams serve as reminders that every part, no matter how broken, holds value and can be integrated into a cohesive, resilient, Self-led whole. When the bowl is whole again, it looks different from before, but it's still beautiful because the client has invested their time into creating each part that represents them. The gold lines remind us that even when something has been hurt, it can be repaired with love and care.

CLIENT EXAMPLE

Ellie, a 17-year-old client, came into therapy overwhelmed by feelings of inadequacy and low self-worth. She was experiencing the ripple effects of prior bullying at school, the dissolution of two long-term friendships, and a recent breakup with her boyfriend. Ellie communicated that she felt broken and unworthy. The kintsugi process became a pivotal intervention in helping her reconnect with her sense of value and with her resilience.

After introducing the activity, Ellie quickly selected a ceramic bowl to represent herself and then, without hesitation, proceeded to immediately break it, expressing feeling just as smashed as the broken bowl itself. Opening the plastic bag and examining the shards and fragments, Ellie began to express her doubt that she could actually repair the bowl. At one point, she noted how much less valuable the bowl was after shattering—it couldn't even be used to hold anything anymore. Ellie's reluctance to begin repairing the bowl reflected her hesitance to engage with the parts of herself that carried pain and shame. This reluctance told me that her protectors were active in this session. Multiple times she stated that the bowl was just too broken or that it wasn't worth fixing.

In the meantime, however, she started the process of decorating her broken pieces. Over the course of two sessions, she talked about the different experiences the parts represented and her beliefs about those parts. She painted the pieces her favorite colors, blue and purple, because they "make her happy," and she wanted to be sure to incorporate them into her bowl. When exploring the materials, Ellie was drawn to a particular swatch of patterned fabric. It had a fairy on it and the phrase "Things are better with glitter." When I asked Ellie what she especially liked about this swatch, she replied that glitter made everything fun and pretty. She then shared that her friends have told her that she makes things fun when she is around.

Over the course of our kintsugi sessions, I watched as Ellie handled each piece, applying glue and carefully filling the cracks with more gold paint. She was clearly becoming increasingly attuned to the experience. Once the bowl was fully repaired, Ellie looked at it with admiration, saying, "Okay. Well, it's not perfect, but, actually, it's better this way. It's stronger now."

Fig. 7.5: Ellie's Kintsugi

By the end of the activity, Ellie's perspective had begun to shift, and her protectors were more relaxed. She was able to share more about her experiences with her old friends and boyfriend. The mended bowl served as an externalized metaphor, allowing Ellie to see her own journey through a different lens, recognizing that the experiences she once believed diminished her worth were instead integral to her growth and identity.

WHY KINTSUGI WORKS

Kintsugi is powerful for many, many clients, but it seems to be especially helpful for clients navigating trauma or loss, likely because it offers a powerful visual metaphor for healing and resilience. Somewhat similarly, it's also valuable for individuals grappling with perfectionism or shame, helping them reframe their perspective on imperfections and see beauty in what was once broken (Kemske, 2021). Clients who process emotions through tactile, embodied creative activities also tend to experience meaningful growth and reflection through this work.

Kintsugi works because it's so adaptable and because it can engage clients physically, emotionally, and symbolically. The process of repairing something broken mirrors the journey of acknowledging pain, taking steps to heal, and embracing a redefined, empowered self. By turning damage into beauty, clients can learn to appreciate their own growth and resilience, transforming their perspective on past struggles into a source of strength and pride. This metaphor frequently transcends the playroom, leaving clients with a lasting image of their capacity for healing and transformation. Children begin to understand that broken things can be mended and that just like the bowl, our hearts and feelings can heal. In addition, cracks tell a story, and instead of hiding what happened, we can use it to grow stronger. Most importantly, we are still whole, even when we feel broken. All of our pieces are still there, ready to put back together with care.

Conclusion

Expressive arts activities like intuitive drawing and kintsugi are not universally suitable for every client or situation, regardless of the therapeutic framework. Even therapists well-versed in play therapy, with a rich repertoire of expressive arts tools at their disposal, recognize that different clients and circumstances call for different approaches. The versatility of expressive arts—such as sandtray, LEGO, or kintsugi—lies in their adaptability. These methods are not bound to specific theoretical models, and this is one reason they're so useful. However, the effectiveness of expressive arts in Playful Parts often depends on the therapist's capacity to engage with curiosity, creativity, and a grounded sense of Self-energy. By attuning to the client's emotional and developmental state, therapists can adapt the activity to align with their unique needs and comfort levels.

It must be stated that even the most effective tools and the most responsive therapists may find that expressive arts activities aren't a fit for every client. While I deeply value and advocate for my Playful Parts activities, applying them often demands creativity—especially when working with clients who are uncomfortable with play, uninterested in engaging, or unable to fully participate. This challenge often comes up with clients grappling with shame tied to the experiences or behaviors that led them to therapy. Those who have endured sexual abuse, witnessed or caused an accident, or experienced neglect are often hesitant to build any kind of connection with their inner parts. They may express deep caution or even suspicion when the subjective of expressive arts activities comes up. Many of these clients have established a fragile sense of stability by relying on a kind of out-of-sight, out-of-mind approach, and relinquishing that coping strategy is rarely something they are ready or willing to do.

But when sandtray, LEGO, and other expressive arts activities resonate with clients, they are powerful tools for unlocking insights, building connections, and facilitating meaningful healing. This is especially the case when we're able to offer our clients significant Self-energy and hold space for their engagement, however it's expressed. If a client shows disinterest or resistance, it's crucial to honor their boundaries and adjust the therapeutic approach accordingly. Staying attuned to the client's preferences and pacing allows the process to unfold naturally. Whether through sandtray, LEGO, or another creative avenue, the goal remains the same—to cultivate a space where clients feel supported and free to explore their inner world in ways that feel authentic and comfortable for them.

PARTS OF ME

We all have parts—some we love and some we do not like so much! Let's see what parts you have!

PARTS OF ME

We all have parts—some we love and some we do not like so much! Let's see what parts you have!

171

CHAPTER 8

Get Playful!

Congratulations, friend! You've journeyed through this book, explored the wonders of IFS and play therapy, and now, here we are—the grand finale. But here's the twist: It's not the end. It's the beginning of a new way to approach your work with kids, families, and even your own playful parts. And most importantly, it's about giving yourself permission to use what you already know, sprinkling in some IFS magic, and trusting your inner therapist to guide the way. Let's dive in.

Embracing Your Inner Playful Part

First things first: If you're going to help clients connect with their playful parts, you've got to get cozy with your own. Yes, you, the grown-up therapist with a calendar full of appointments and a shelf full of therapy books. Somewhere inside you, there's a part that loves to get silly, curious, and creative. Maybe it shows up when you doodle during meetings or bust out a ridiculous dance move when nobody's looking. Or maybe it's been waiting for an invitation to come out and play. Consider this your invitation.

When you let your playful part take the lead in sessions, something magical happens. Your energy shifts, and suddenly, your clients—no matter how young or old—feel the freedom to explore their own playful sides. You model the kind of openness and curiosity that are at the heart of both play therapy and IFS. So, don't overthink it. Grab that puppet, make that silly sound, and let your playful part remind you why you love this work.

The Power of Playful Parts

In IFS, we talk a lot about parts—the protectors, the exiles—and, of course, the Self. But what about the parts that love to giggle, explore, and create? These playful parts are often the key to unlocking healing, especially in kids. They can disarm even the most guarded protectors and bring a sense of safety and joy to the therapeutic process.

Here's a tip: When working with a child (or an adult!) who seems stuck, invite their playful part to join the conversation. You can do this directly ("I wonder if there's a part of you that likes to have fun . . . What would it say right now?") or indirectly by introducing a playful activity. Sandtray, expressive arts, or even just a game of catch can create the space for these parts to show up and share their wisdom. The sandtray in particular is a small but mighty tool in the world of play therapy. When you join it with IFS, it becomes even more powerful. Think of the sandtray as a stage where parts can come to life. Those tiny figures and symbols? They're not just toys; they're storytellers. Remember, you have the ability to set the stage not only for the clients you serve but also for yourself. I invite you to create a world that represents how you are feeling or what's happening inside of you. I remind you—just as we remind our clients—that there's no right or wrong way to do it.

Beyond sandtray, remember that the expressive arts—whether it's painting, drawing, sculpting, or making music—are like a direct line to the Self. They bypass the logical brain and let parts express themselves in ways that words can't. Plus, they're fun. And let's be honest, we all need a little more fun in our lives. Here's the deal: You don't have to be an artist to use expressive arts in therapy. You just have to be willing to get messy. Keep a stash of supplies handy—markers, clay, pipe cleaners, whatever sparks joy—and let the client's parts guide the process.

If there's one thing I want you to take away from this book, it's this: You already have everything you need to integrate Playful Parts into your therapy practice. The techniques you love? Keep using them. Just add a dash of parts awareness and a sprinkle of Self-energy. Trust that your playful part knows what it's doing. Trust that your client's parts will show up exactly as they need to. And trust that healing doesn't have to be serious to be profound. So, go forth and play. Build worlds in the sand. Paint outside the lines. Let your playful part guide the way. Because when you give yourself permission to play, you give your clients permission to heal.

Why Expand Beyond Kids?

Let's face it: Play and creativity aren't just for little ones. Parents, families, and even couples are navigating their own inner worlds, complete with parts that could use some nurturing. A parent can learn to meet their "inner critic" with the same kindness they show their child. A family can create new patterns through collaborative storytelling or shared activities. A couple can discover playful ways to reconnect and rebuild trust. You're already equipped to help these folks—Playful Parts can help you meet *anyone* where they're at, no matter their age.

At this point, you might be thinking, *But I only work with kids* or *Play therapy isn't for couples.* But the thing is, growth happens in the stretch. You don't have to be perfect or know every single intervention before you try. Trust yourself, trust your training, and trust your clients—they'll guide you if you let them. You can start small. Invite a parent into a session and let them witness their child's world through play. Try using a simple metaphor or storytelling activity with a couple to explore their relationship dynamics. Dip your toes into family sculpting or creating shared visualizations to bring everyone's parts into the room. It doesn't have to be complicated to be effective.

As you step into this work, hold onto one very important truth: every family, couple, and individual is unique. Culture, language, traditions, and values shape how people connect, process, and heal. That means you need to show up with humility and curiosity—and sometimes adjust your approach—as one size does not fit all. When working with diverse populations, ask yourself:

- How does culture shape their views on play, family roles, or emotions?
- What symbols or materials will resonate most deeply with *them*?
- How can I use their strengths, traditions, and language to build rapport?

This isn't about being perfect or knowing everything—it's about being present and adaptable.

Let's Play (for Real!)

Before you panic and think, *But I don't have a Pinterest-worthy playroom with shelves full of toys and sandtray miniatures spilling onto the floor!*—relax. You don't need it. Yes, those tools are fantastic, but the heart of this work isn't about the stuff; it's about **connection**, **creativity**, and **curiosity**. Whether you have a fancy setup or just a handful of dollar-store treasures, you already have everything you need.

This is your invitation to explore, experiment, and have a little fun. Dust off those old board games. Grab some puppets or crayons. Don't underestimate the power of silly voices or creating imaginary "parts" for everyday objects. Even something as simple as a shared laugh can open doors you didn't even know were there. Whether you're working with a 5-year-old, a 45-year-old, or an entire family of five, remember this: Play isn't a luxury—it's a universal language. And you, brave therapist, are fluent. Now, let's go make some magic. What do you think? Ready to play outside the box?

Remember, you have permission to play.

REFERENCES

Anderson, F. G., Sweezy, M., & Schwartz, R. C. (2017). *Internal family systems skills training manual: Trauma-informed treatment for anxiety, depression, PTSD & substance abuse.* PESI Publishing & Media.

Axline, V. M. (1947). *Play therapy.* Ballantine Books.

Axline, V. M. (1964). *Dibs in search of self.* Ballantine Books.

Haas, S. C., & Ray, D. C. (2020). Child-centered play therapy with children affected by adverse childhood experiences: A single-case design. *International Journal of Play Therapy, 29*(4), 223–236. https://doi.org/10.1037/pla0000135

Hinz, L. D. (2020). *Expressive therapies continuum: A framework for using art in therapy* (2nd ed.). Routledge.

Homeyer, L. E. (2019). *The history of sand therapy.* World Association of Sand Therapy Professionals. https://worldsandtherapy.org/page/Contemporaries

Homeyer, L. E., & Sweeney, D. S. (2022). *Sandtray therapy: A practical manual* (4th ed.). Routledge.

Hori, M. (2022). *A beginner's guide to kintsugi: The Japanese art of repairing pottery and glass.* Tuttle Publishing.

Kaduson, H. G., & Schaefer, C. E. (Eds.). (2016). *Play therapy with children: Modalities for change.* American Psychological Association.

Kalff, D. (1980). *Sandplay: A psychotherapeutic approach to the psyche.* Sigo Press.

Kemske, B. (2021). *Kintsugi: The Poetic Mend.* Herbert Press.

Kestly, T. A. (2014). *The interpersonal neurobiology of play: Brain-building interventions for emotional well-being.* W. W. Norton & Company

Kristiansen, P., & Rasmussen, R. (2014). *Building a better business using the LEGO® SERIOUS PLAY® method.* Wiley.

Kottman, T., & Meany-Walen, K. (2016). *Partners in play: An Adlerian approach to play therapy.* (3rd ed). American Counseling Association.

Landreth, G. L. (2024). *Play therapy: The art of the relationship* (4th ed.). Routledge.

LeGoff, D. B., Gómez de la Cuesta, G., Krauss, G. W., & Baron-Cohen, S. (2014). *LEGO®-based therapy: How to build social competence through LEGO®-based clubs for children with autism and related conditions.* Jessica Kingsley Publishers.

Lowenfeld, M. (1979). *The world technique.* Allen & Unwin.

Malchiodi, C. A. (2003). *The art therapy sourcebook.* McGraw Hill.

Parmalee, H., & Schwartz, R. C. (2023). Overview, origins, and future of the IFS model. In J. Riemersma (Ed.), *Altogether us: Integrating the IFS model with key modalities, communities, and trends* (pp. 3–19). Pivotal Press.

Rubin, J. A. (2016). *Approaches to art therapy: Theory and technique* (3rd ed.). Routledge.

Schaefer, C. E., & Drewes, A. A. (Eds.). (2013). *The therapeutic powers of play: 20 core agents of change* (2nd ed). Wiley.

Schwartz, R. C. (2021). *No bad parts: Healing trauma and restoring wholeness with the internal family systems model.* Sounds True.

Schwartz, R. C. (2023). *Introduction to the internal family systems model.* Trailheads Publications.

Schwartz, R. C., & Sweezy, M. (2020). *Internal family systems therapy* (2nd ed.). The Guilford Press.

Senko, K., & Harper, B. (2019). Play therapy: An illustrative case. *Innovations in Clinical Neuroscience, 16*(5–6), 38–40.

Spiegel, L. (2017). *Internal family systems with children.* Routledge

Turns, B., Springer, P., Eddy, B. P., & Sibley, D. S. (2021). "Your exile is showing": Integrating sandtray with internal family systems therapy. *American Journal of Family Therapy, 49*(1), 74–90. https://doi.org/10.1080/01926187.2020.1851617

Wells, H. G. (1911). *Floor games.* Frank Palmer.

ABOUT THE AUTHOR

Carmen Jimenez-Pride is a trailblazing mental health professional, award-winning and best-selling children's book author, and the visionary creator of Focus on Feelings®— an emotional literacy program and product line transforming how clinicians and educators support emotional development.

With over two decades of experience, Carmen brings a wealth of expertise to the field. She is a licensed clinical social worker, Registered Play Therapist Supervisor, certified EMDR therapist and consultant, certified Internal Family Systems (IFS) therapist, and solo lead trainer with the IFS Institute. Her additional credentials include certified AutPlay® therapy provider, registered children's yoga teacher, internationally credentialed sandtray therapist, certified LEGO® SERIOUS PLAY® facilitator, certified Daring Way™ facilitator, and licensed trainer for Training from the BACK of the Room—both in-person and virtually.

Carmen's clinical work is deeply rooted in trauma-informed care and creative expression. She integrates modalities such as brainspotting and Adlerian play therapy to support clients across the lifespan. Known for her ability to make complex theory approachable and actionable, she inspires both new and seasoned therapists through hands-on, engaging trainings.

She is a sought-after international speaker, business consultant, and creator of impactful tools and programs that help clinicians elevate their practice. Carmen's contributions to the field were recognized with the 2021 Association for Play Therapy Emerging Leader Award.

Carmen currently serves on the South Carolina Association for Play Therapy Board, the EMDR International Association, and as the ICST Provider Liaison with the International Sandtray Therapy Association. She is also the founder of Diversity in Play Therapy Inc., where she leads initiatives to enhance training and access for professionals in the field.

Carmen's commitment to excellence and innovation has positioned her as a leading voice in play therapy, EMDR, and IFS—redefining what it means to do meaningful, lasting clinical work with children, teens, and families.